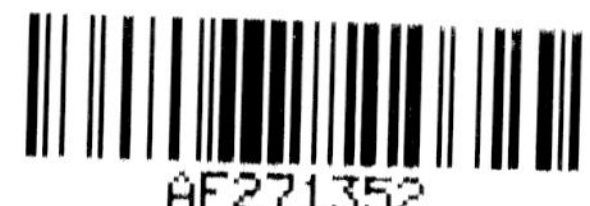

FÉLINS FASCINANTS

Adulte Edition De Chats A Colorier

Coloring Bandit

Publié par Speedy Publishing Canada Limited

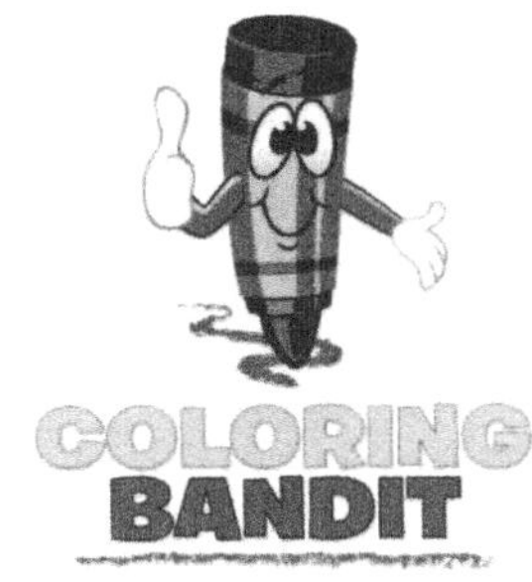

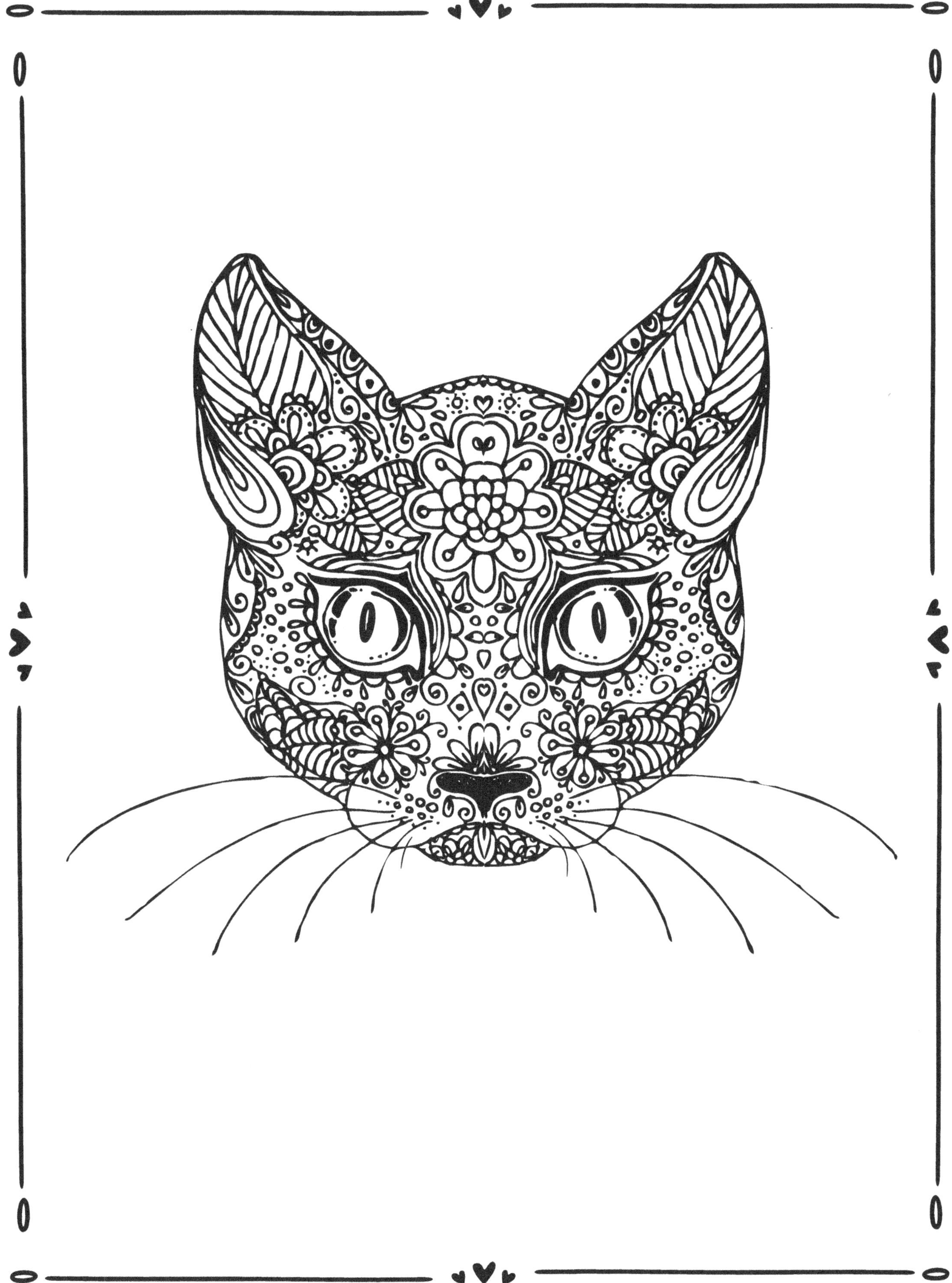

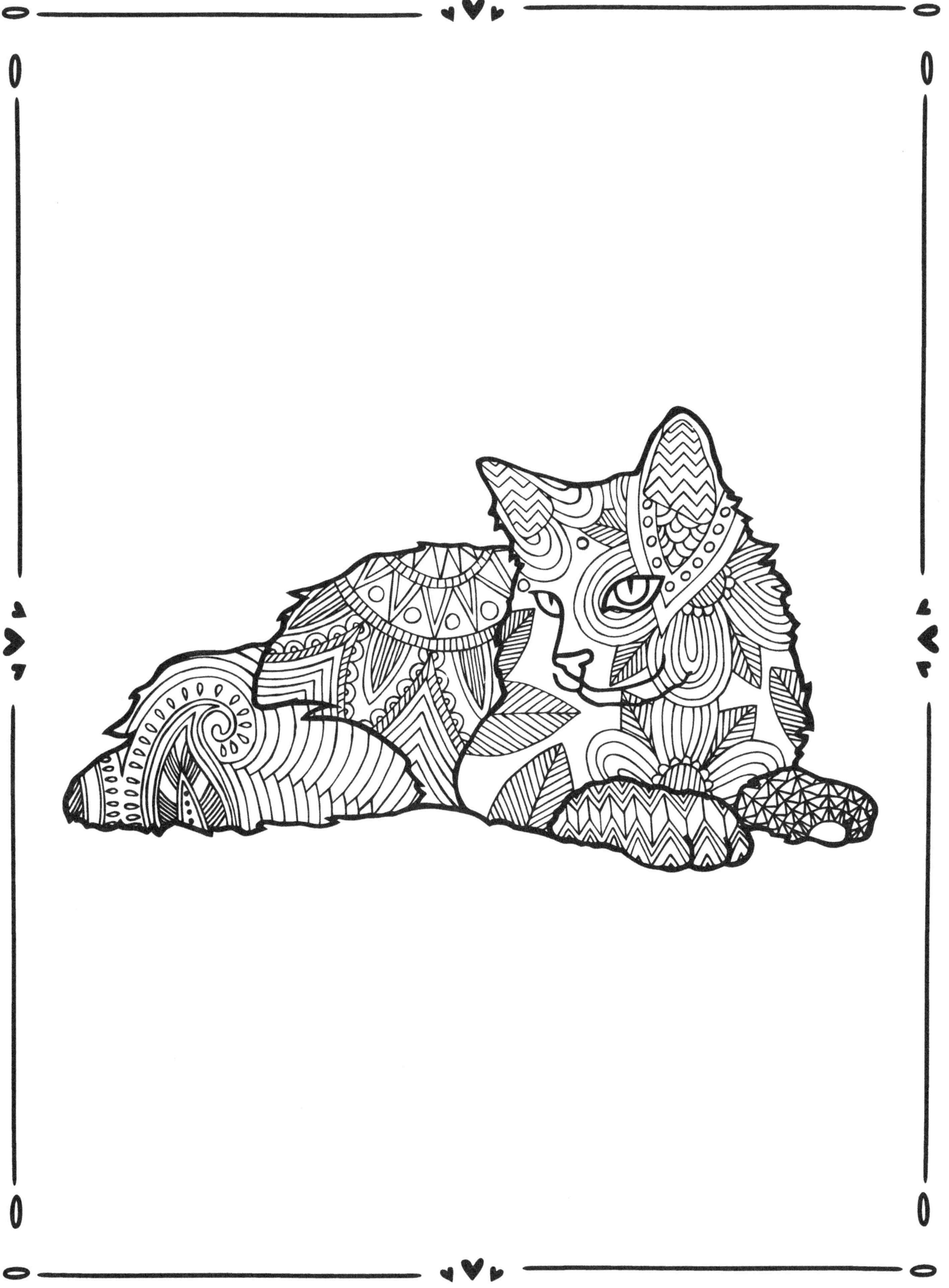

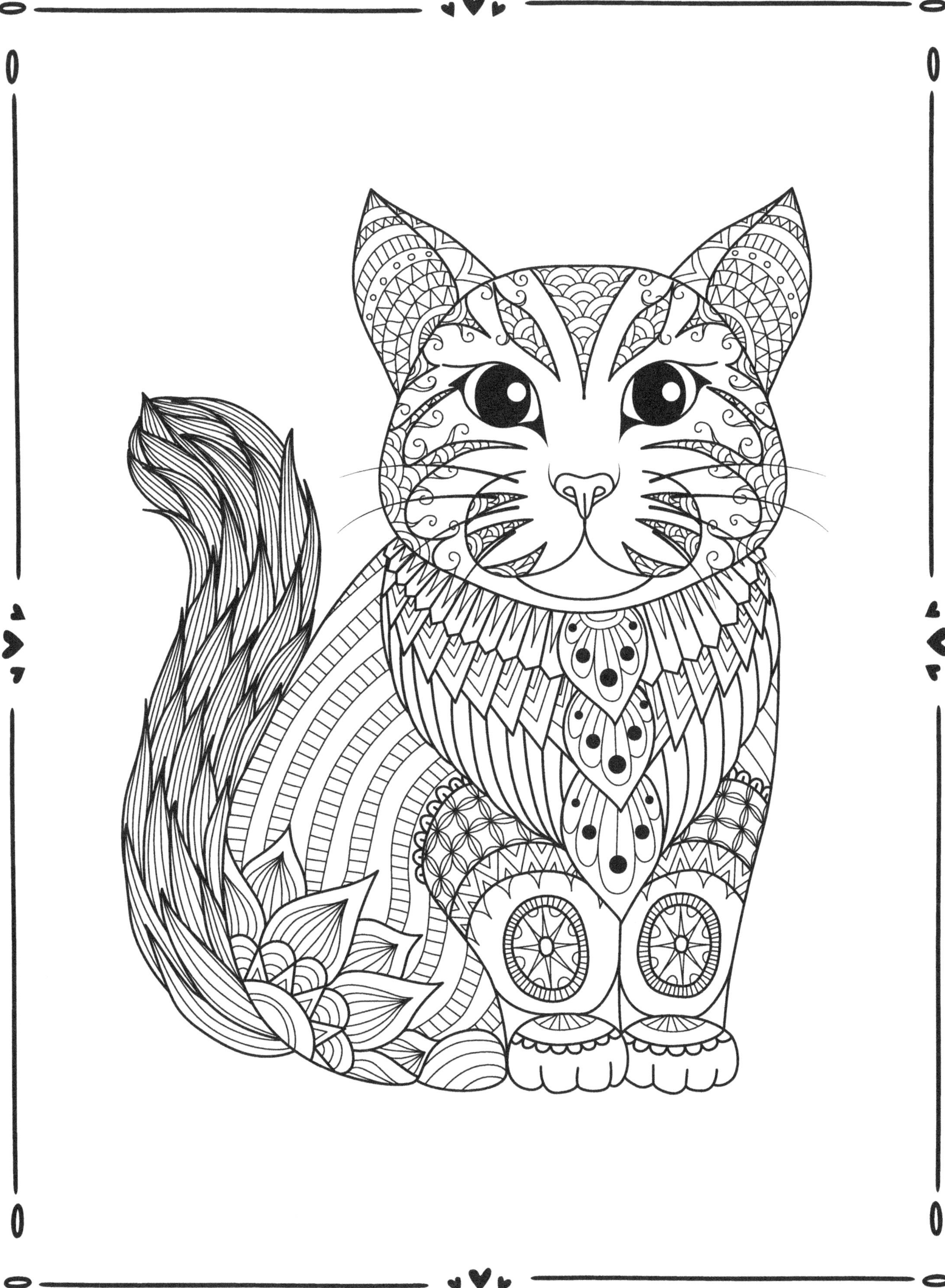

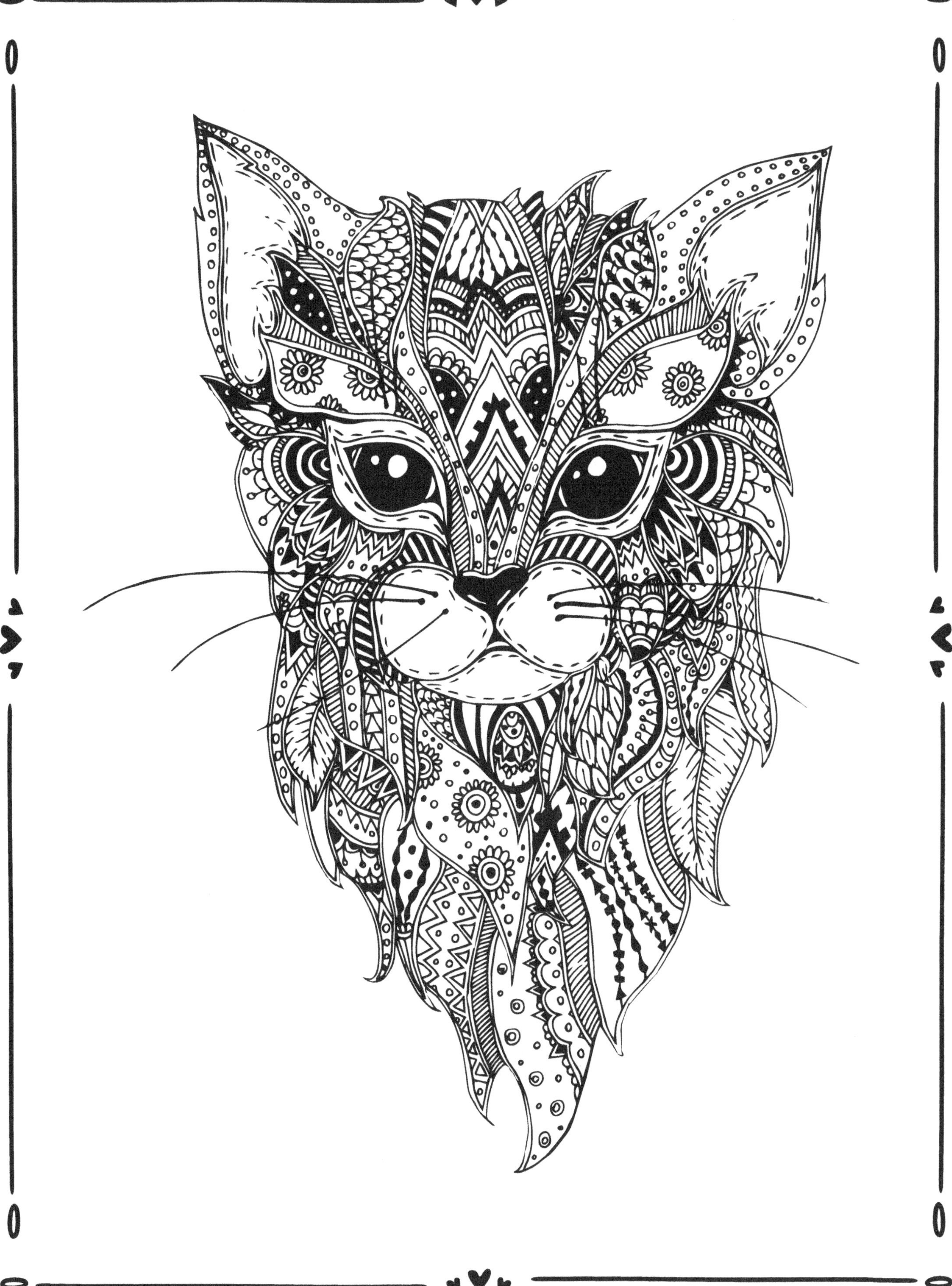

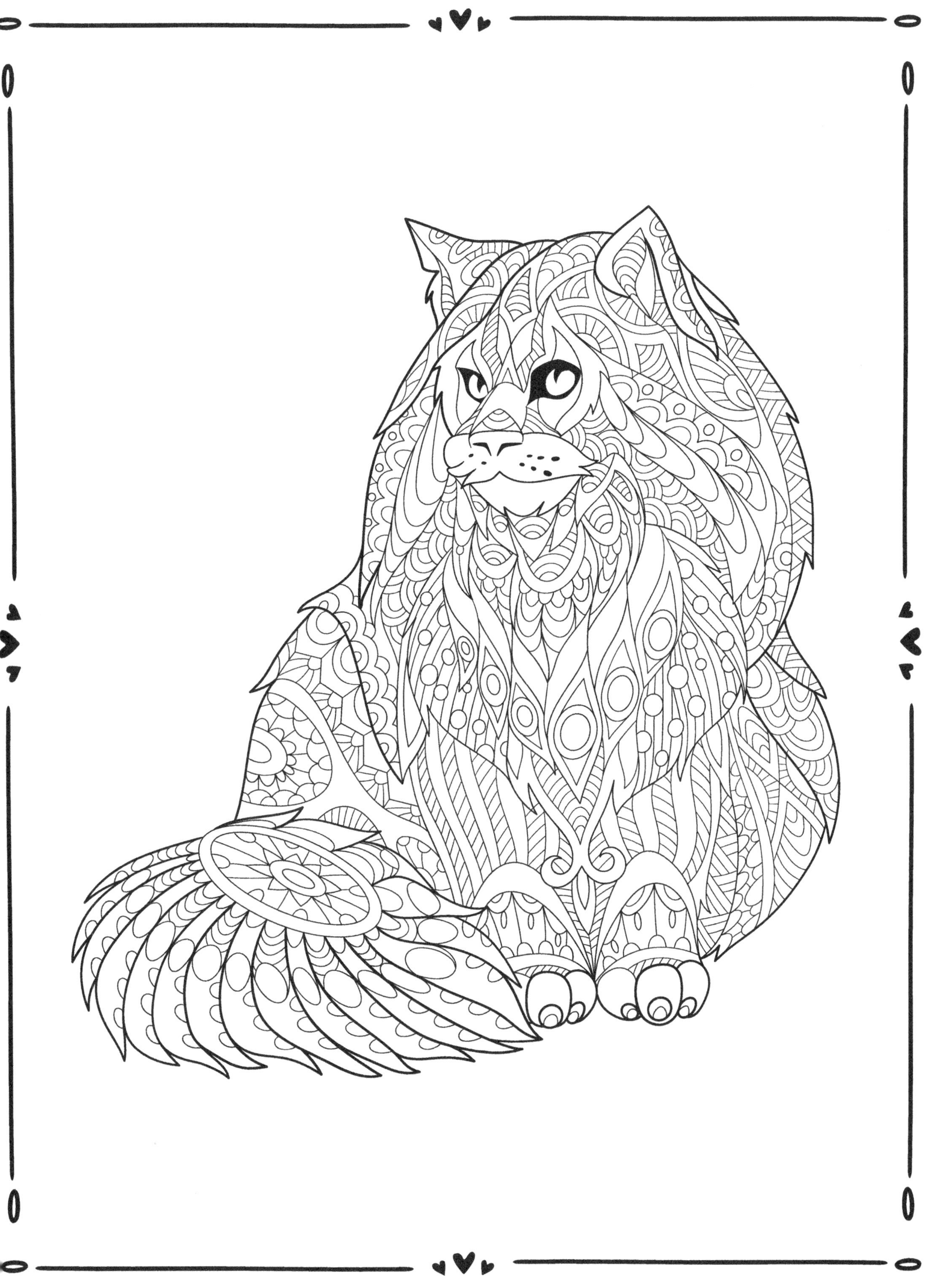

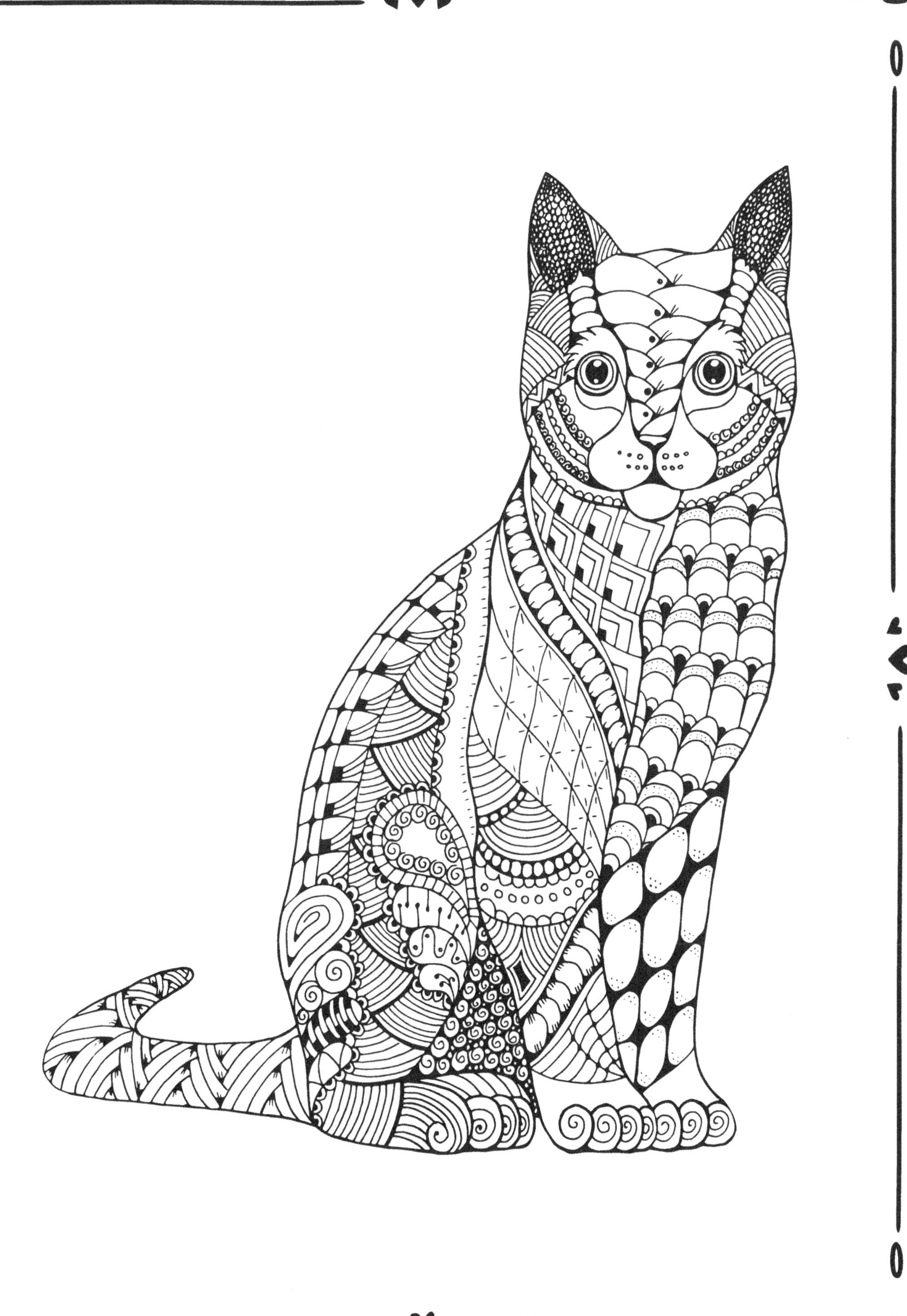

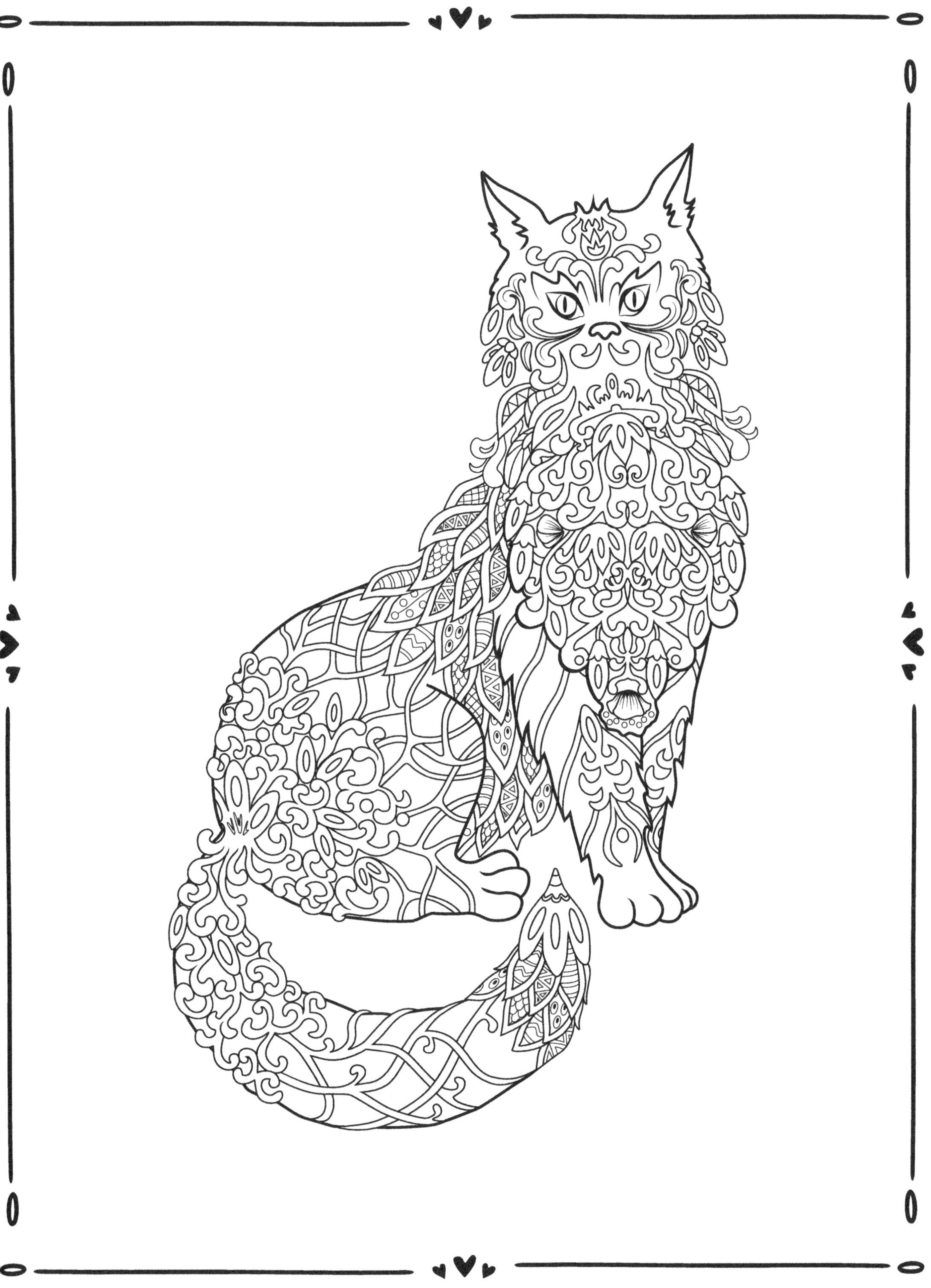

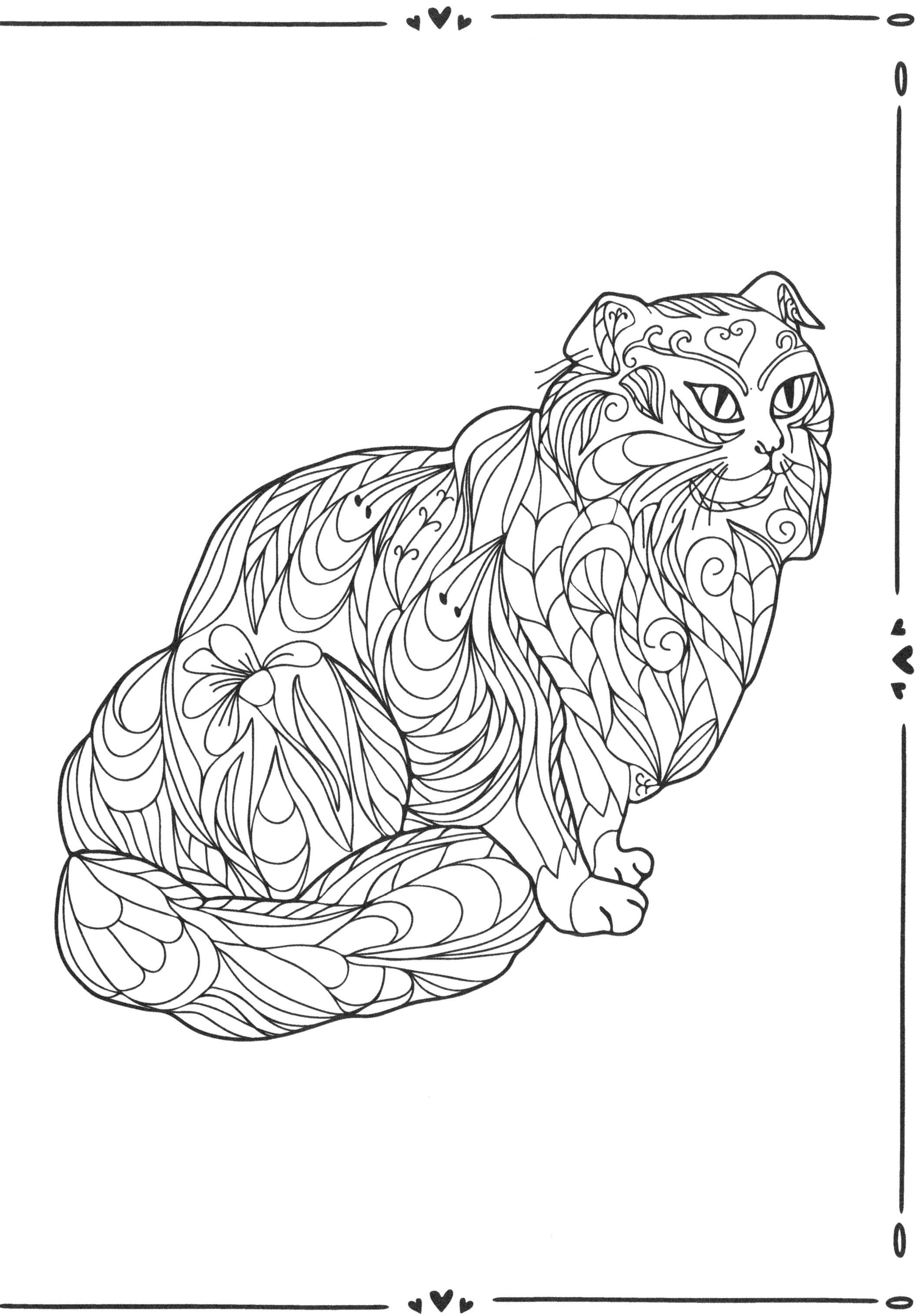

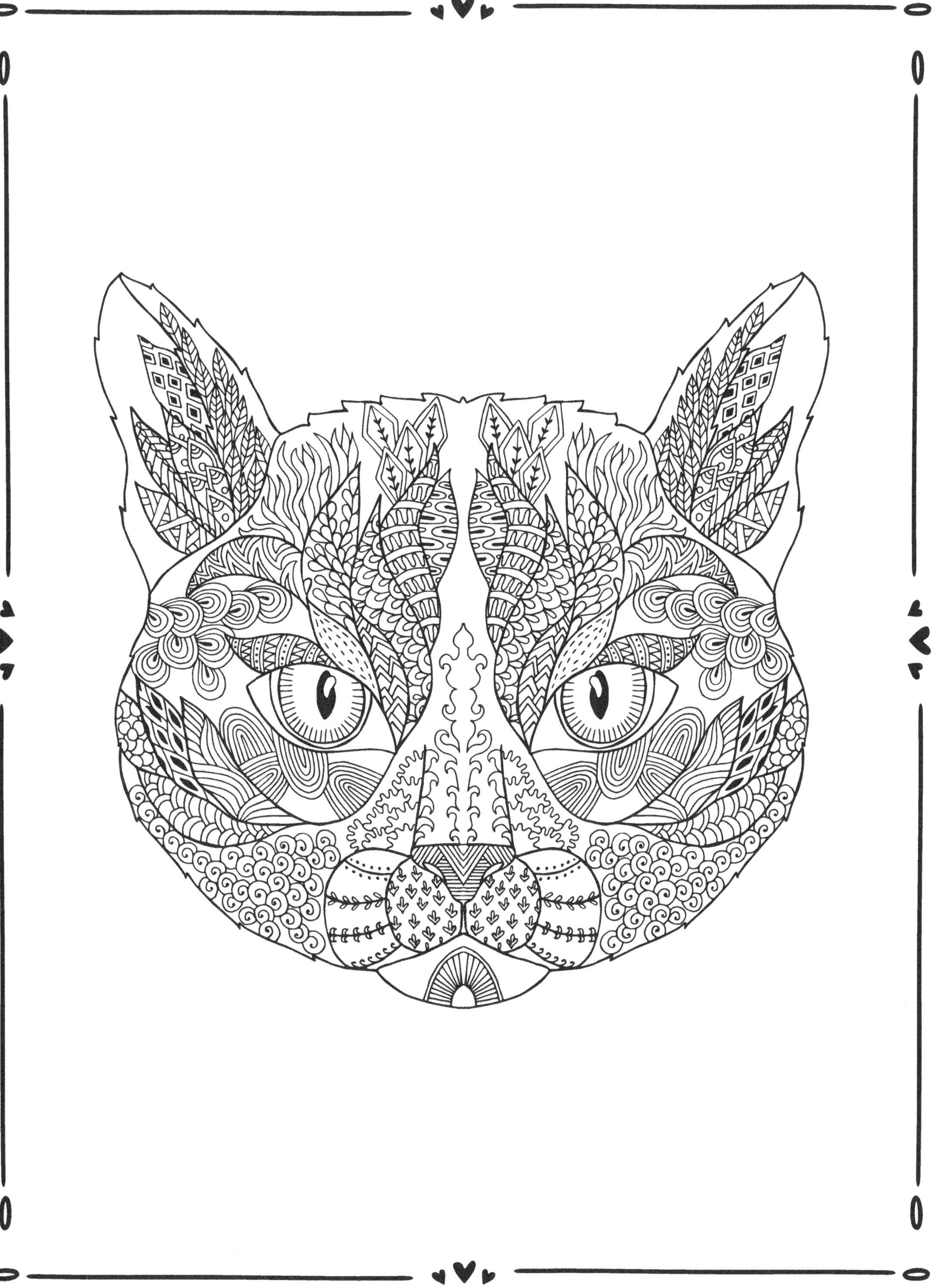

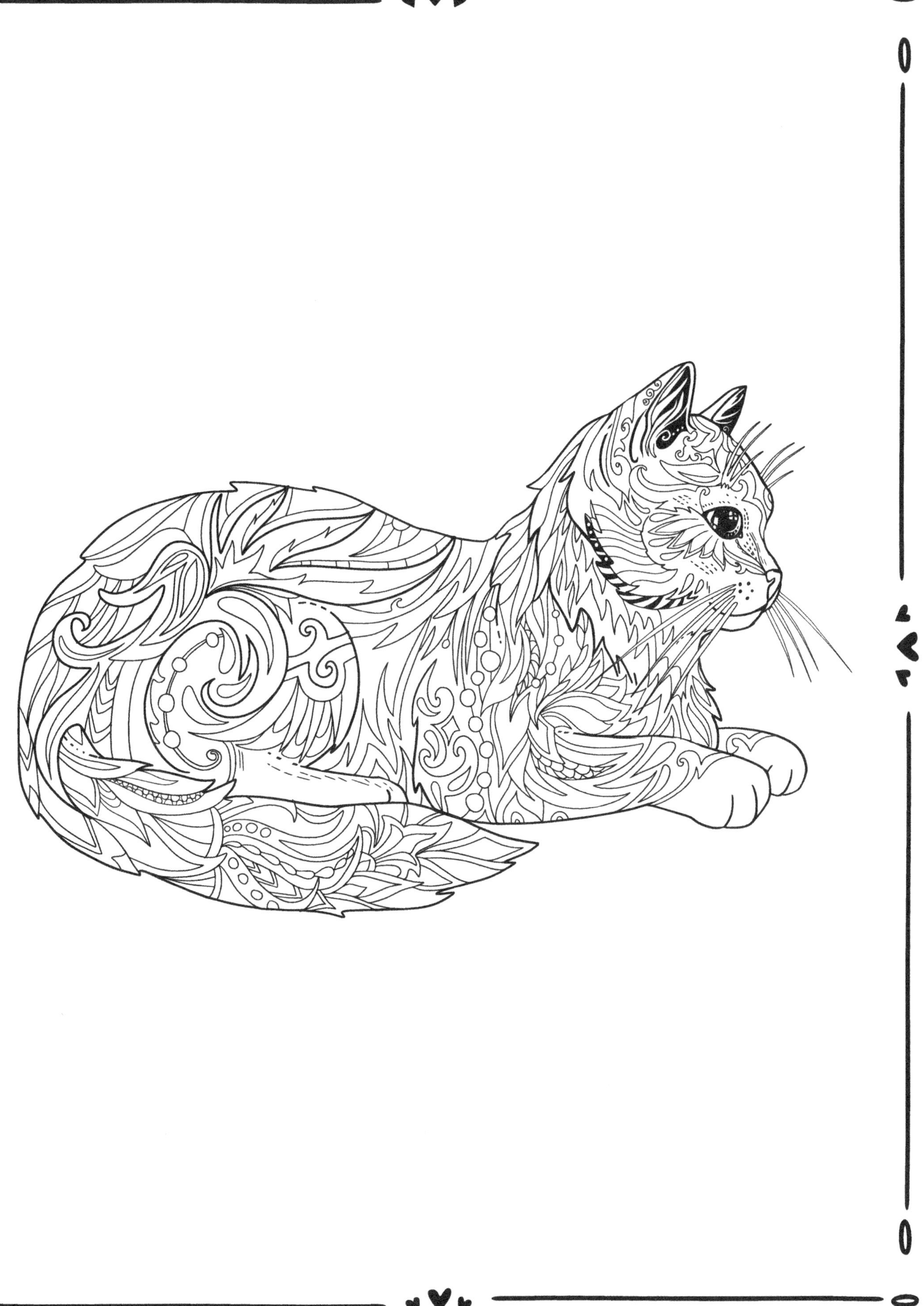

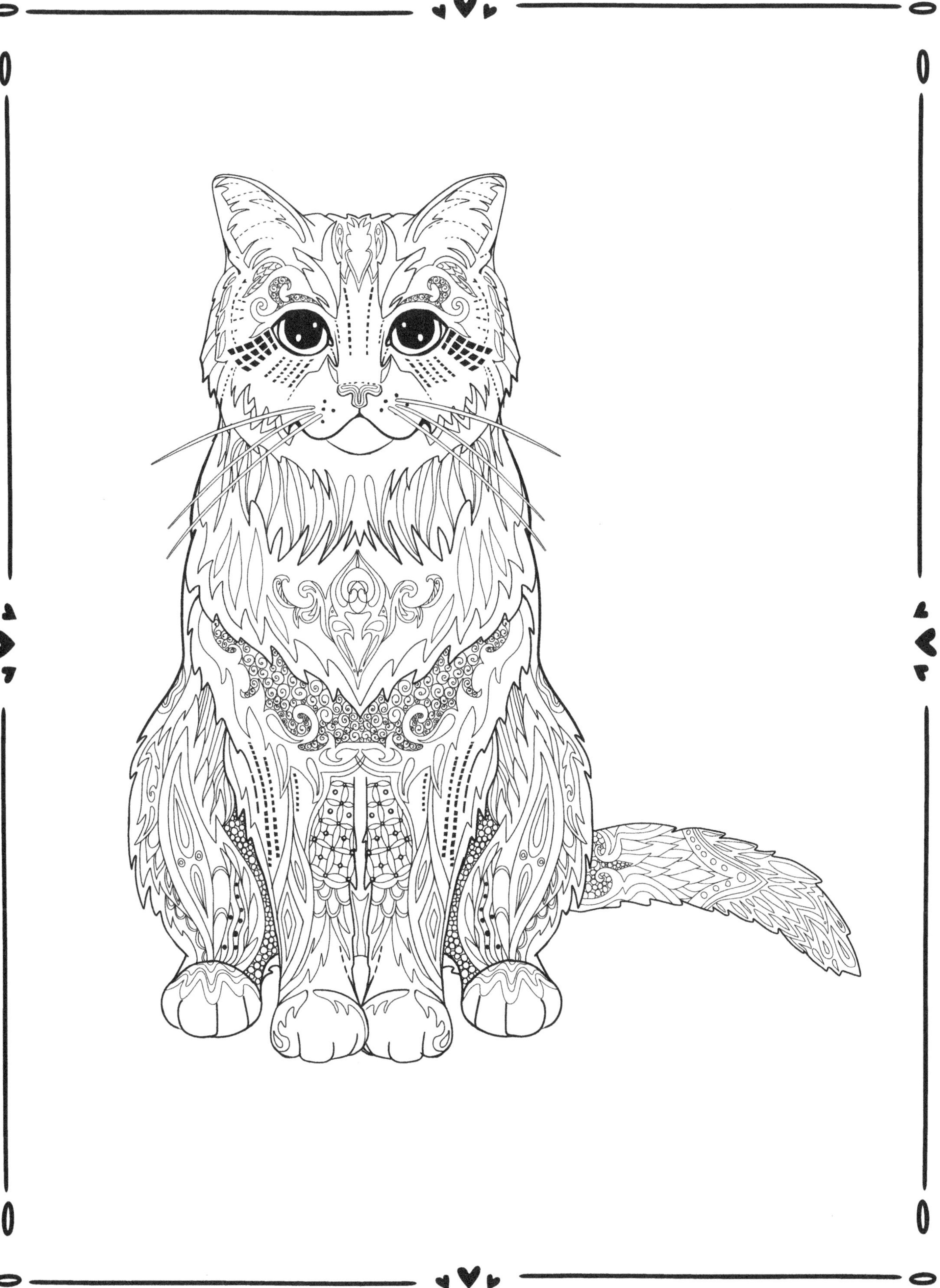

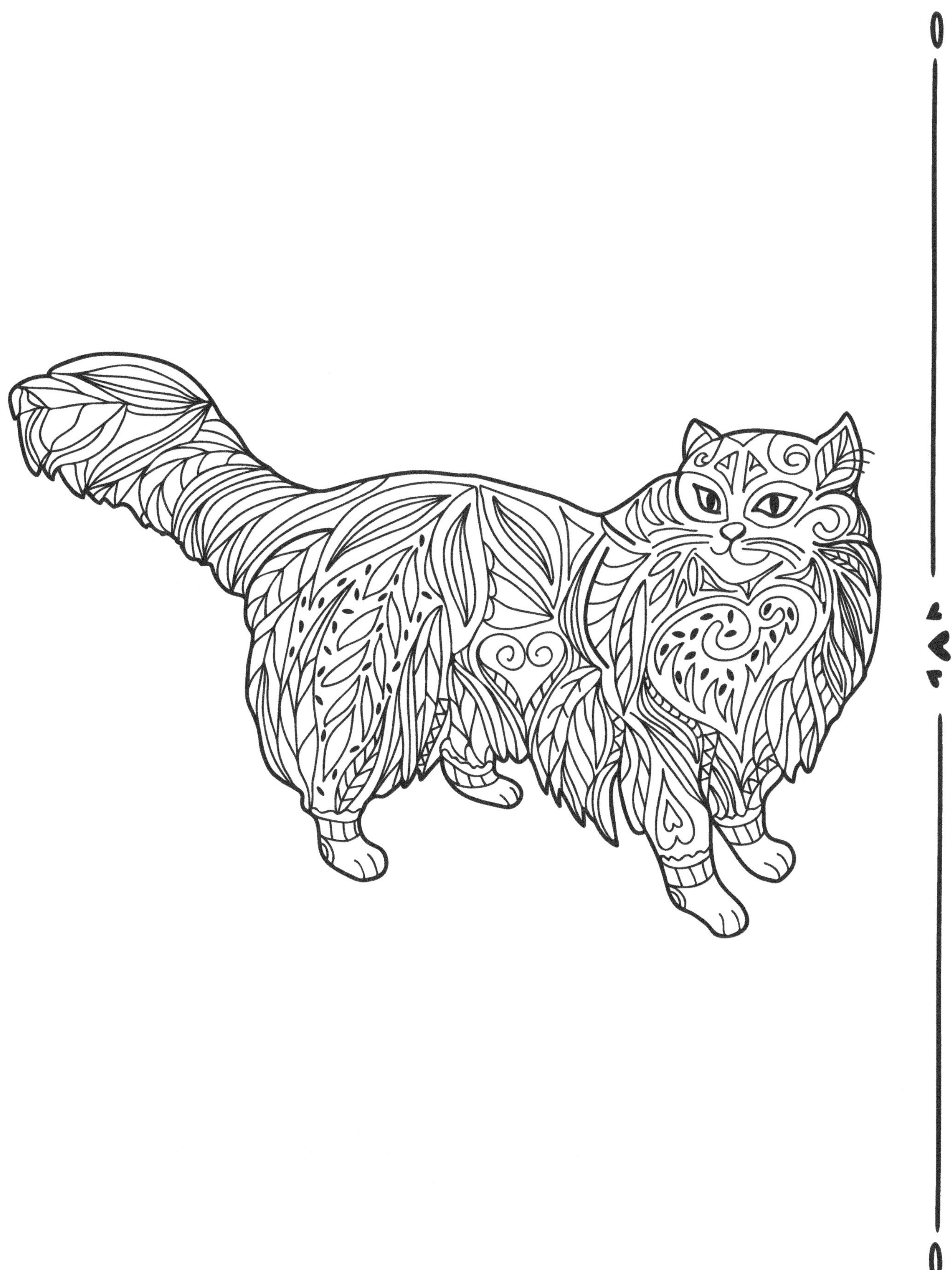

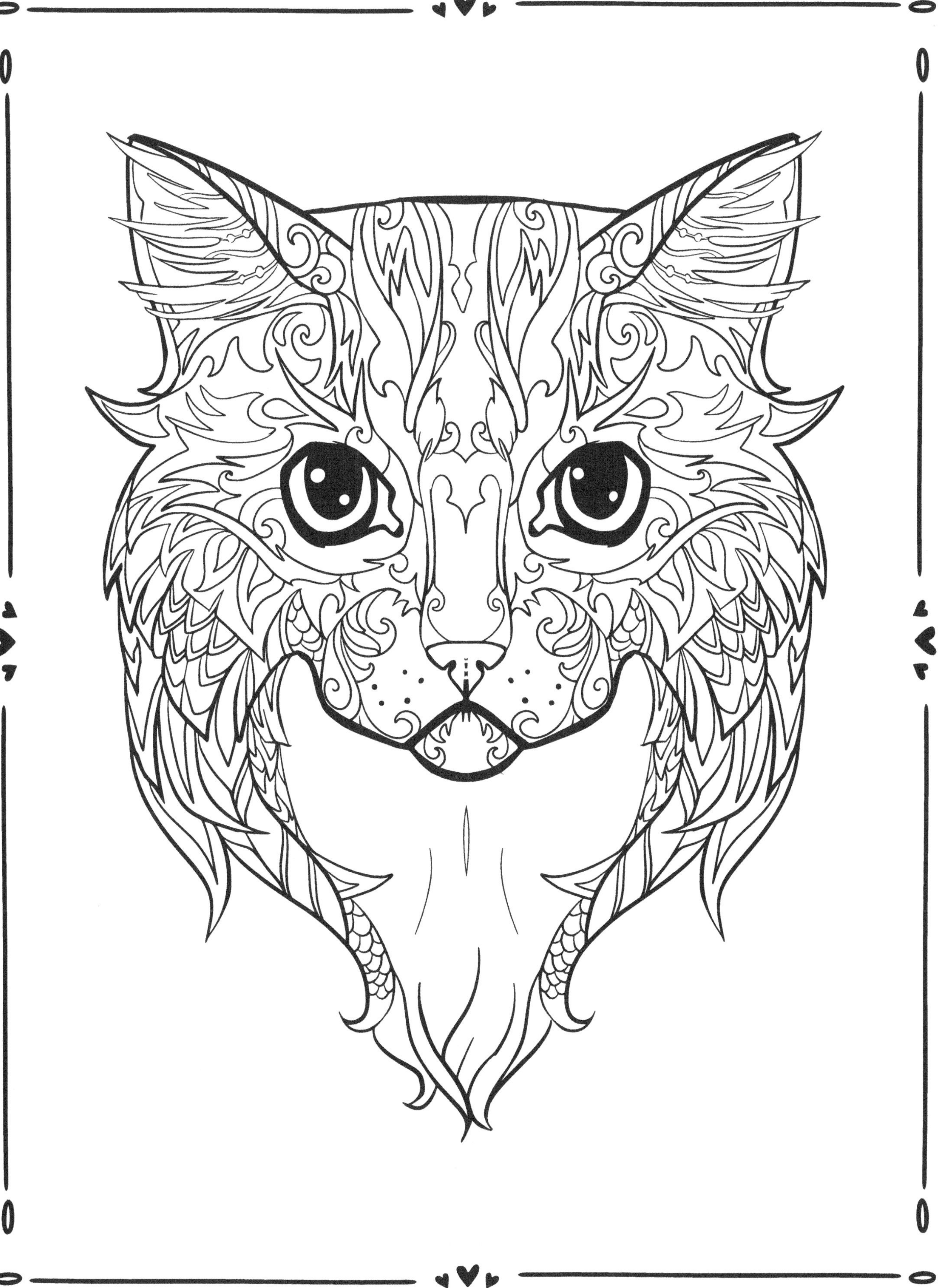

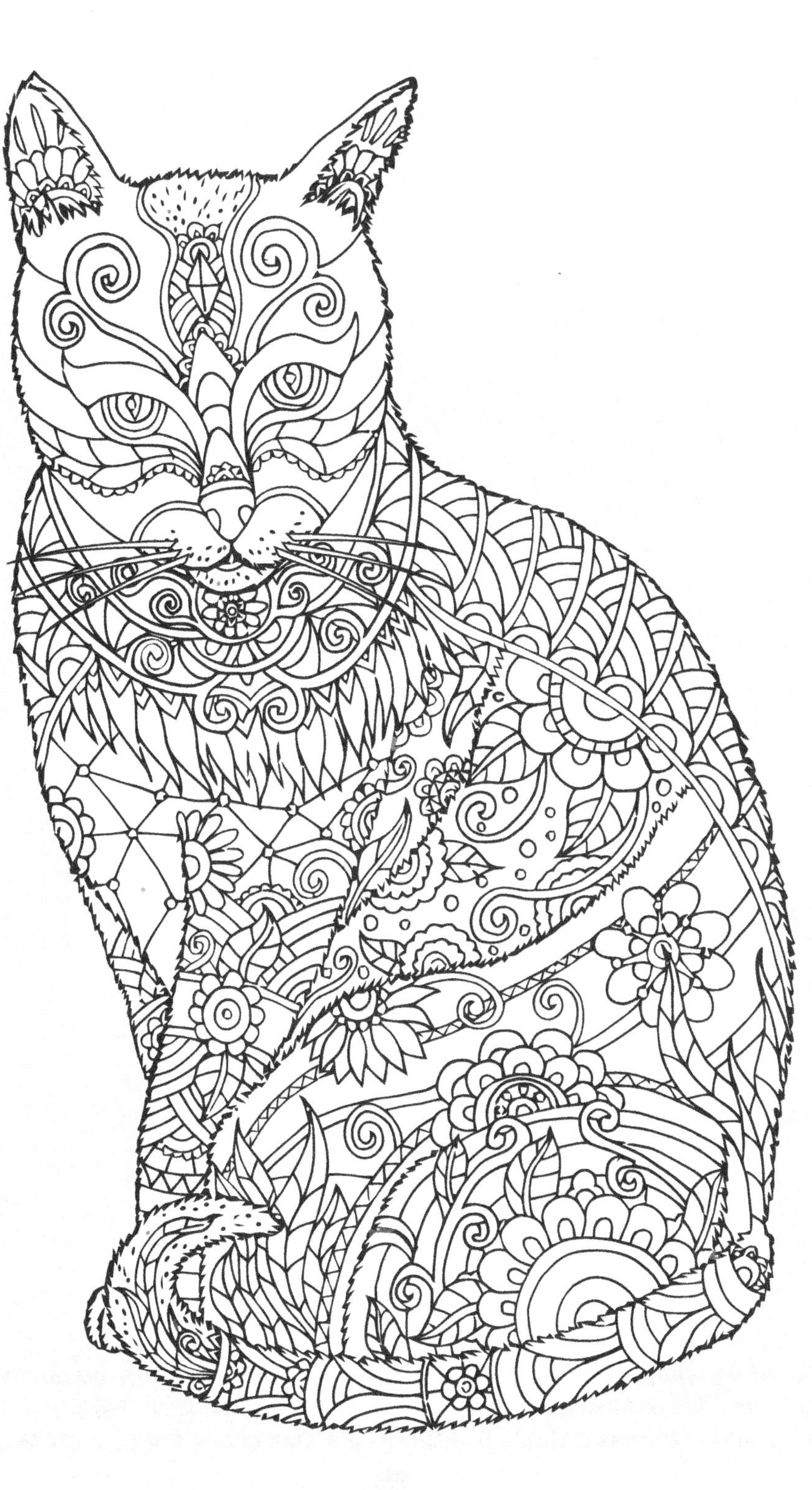

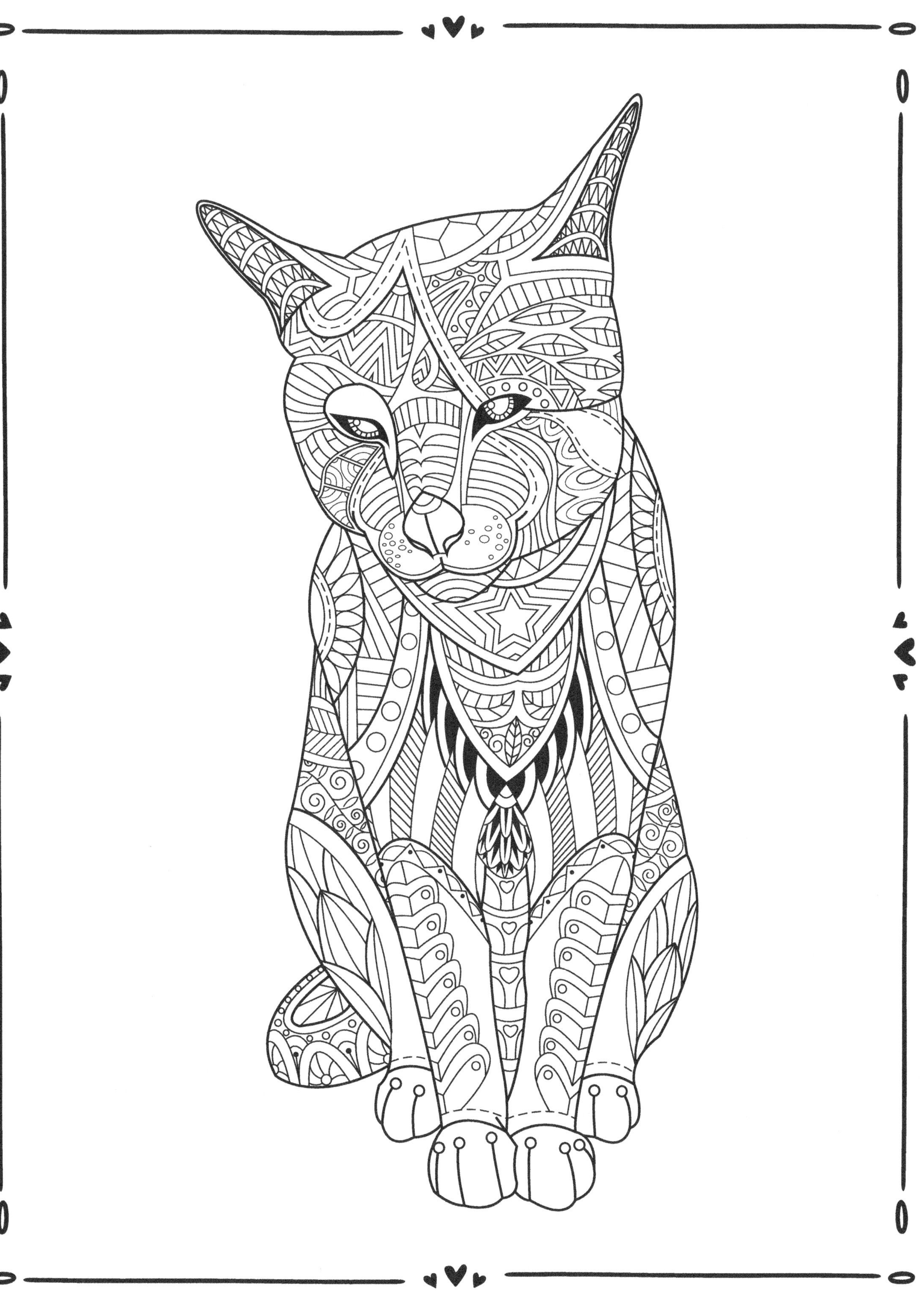

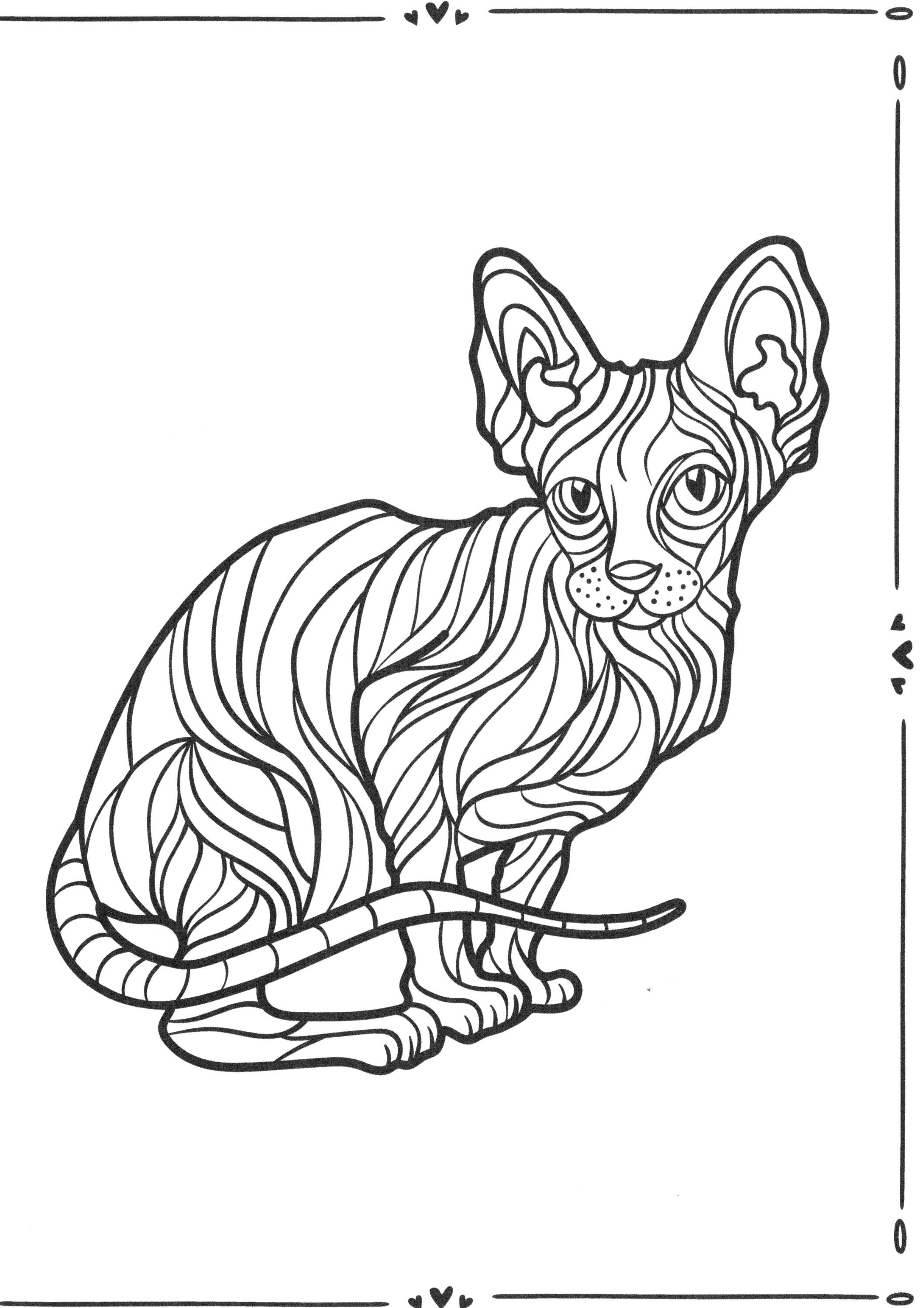

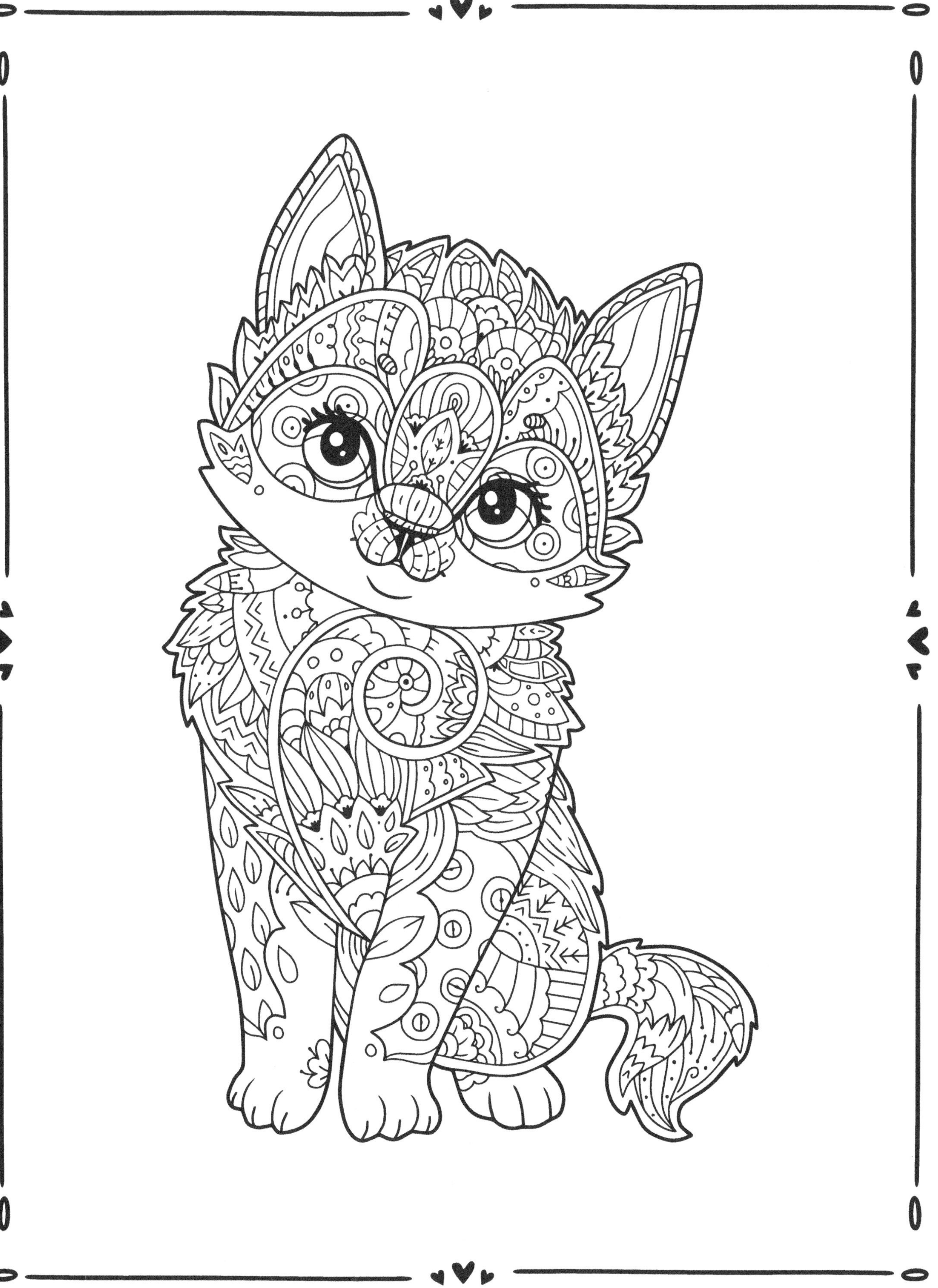

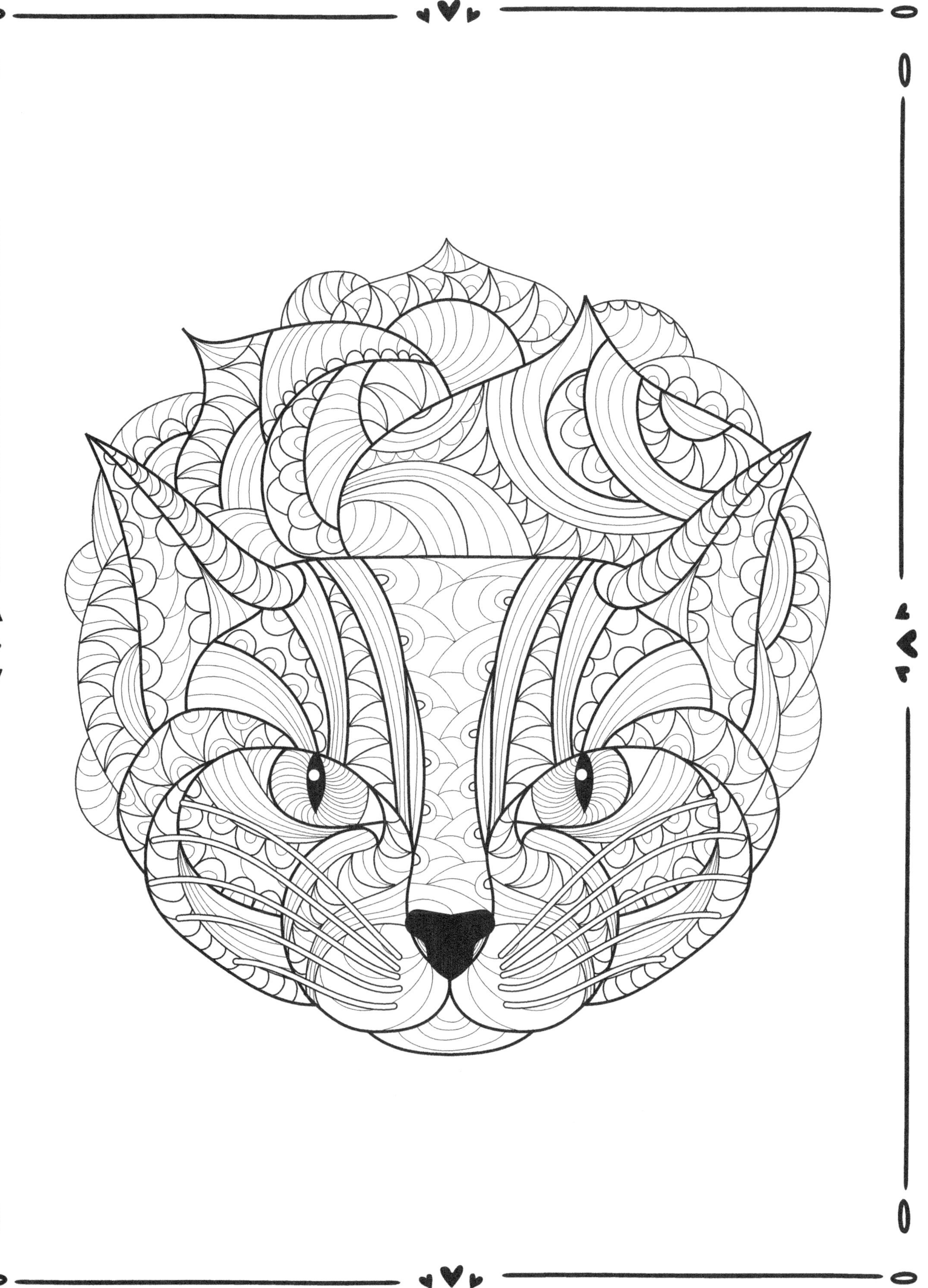

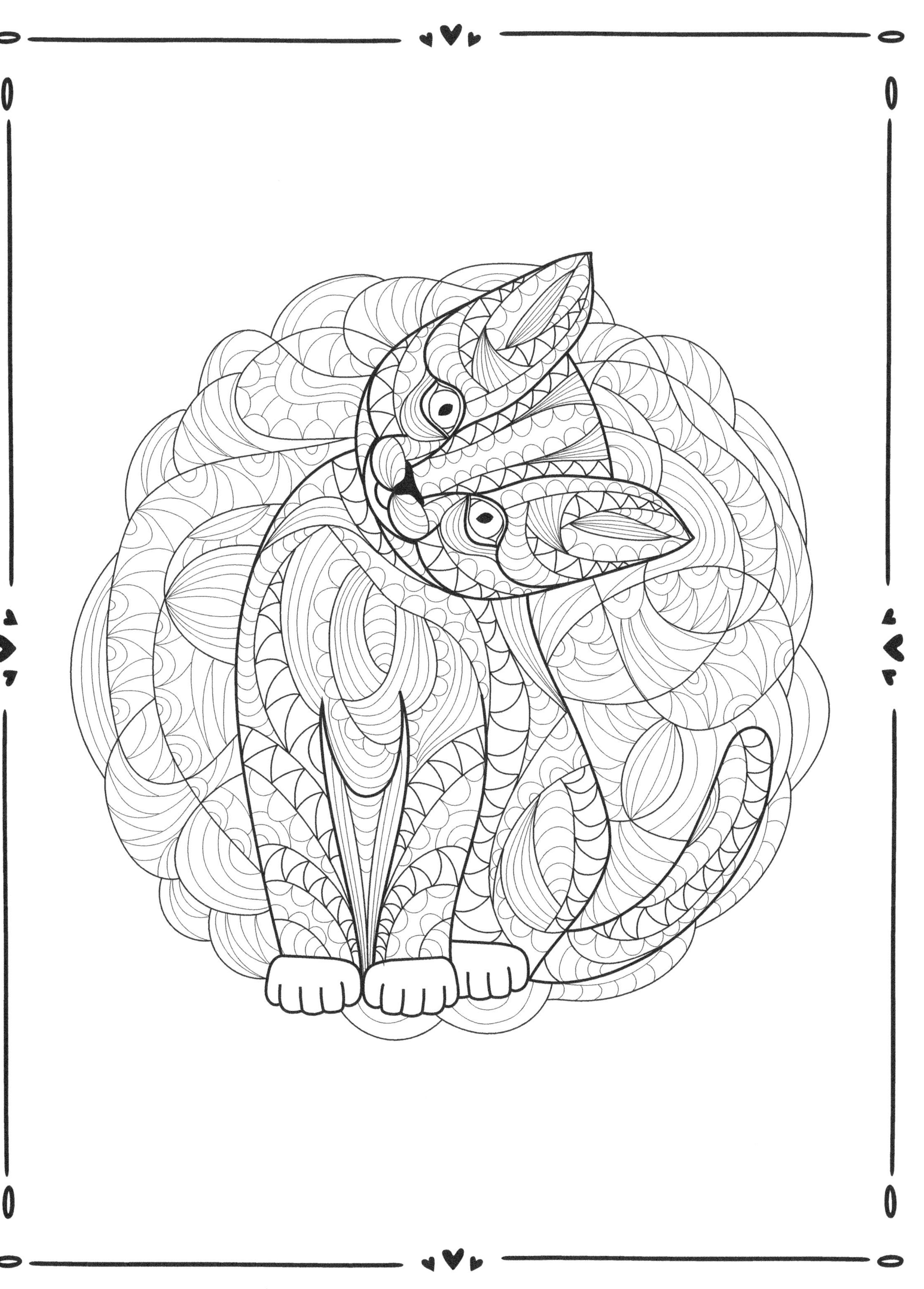

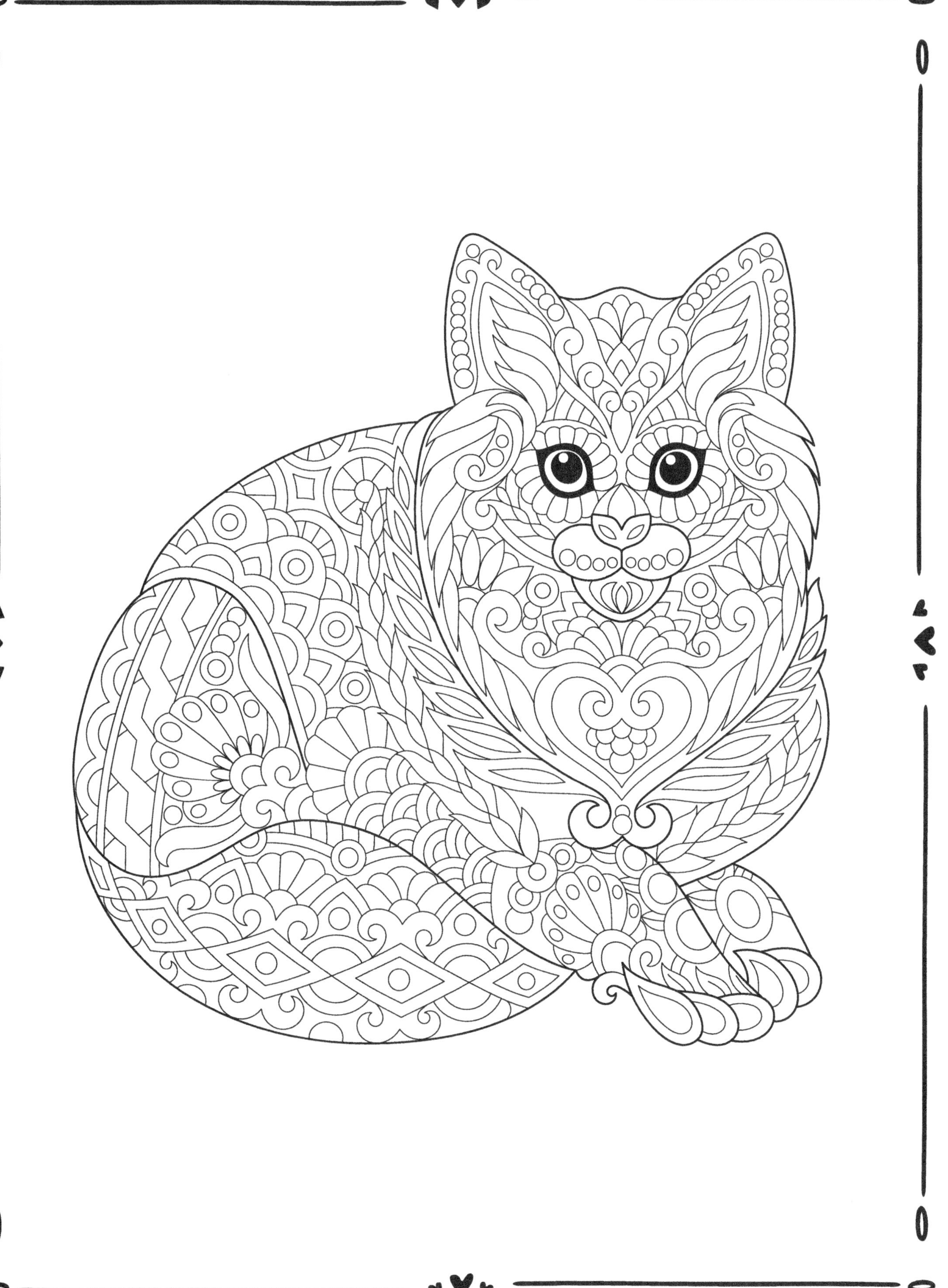

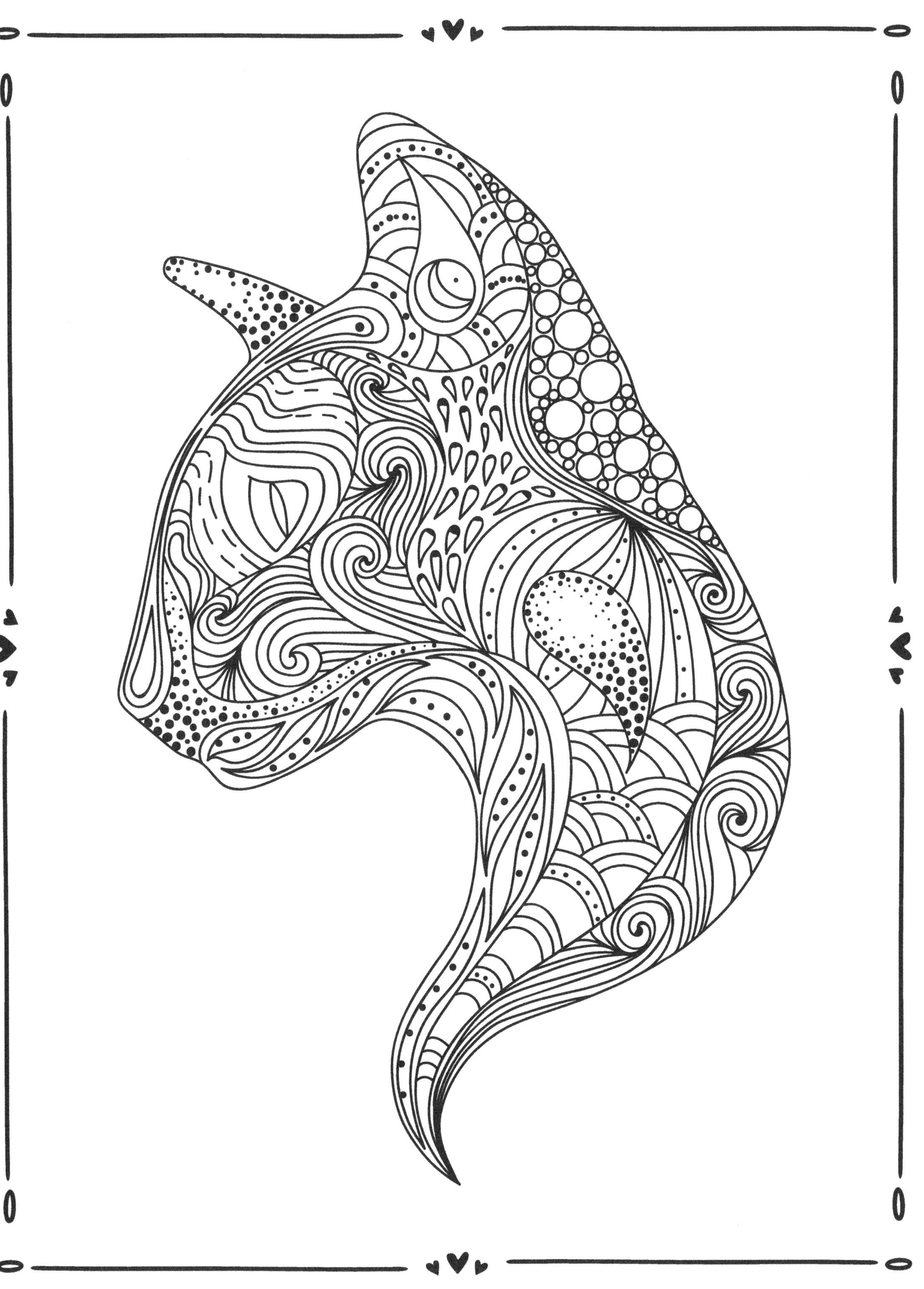

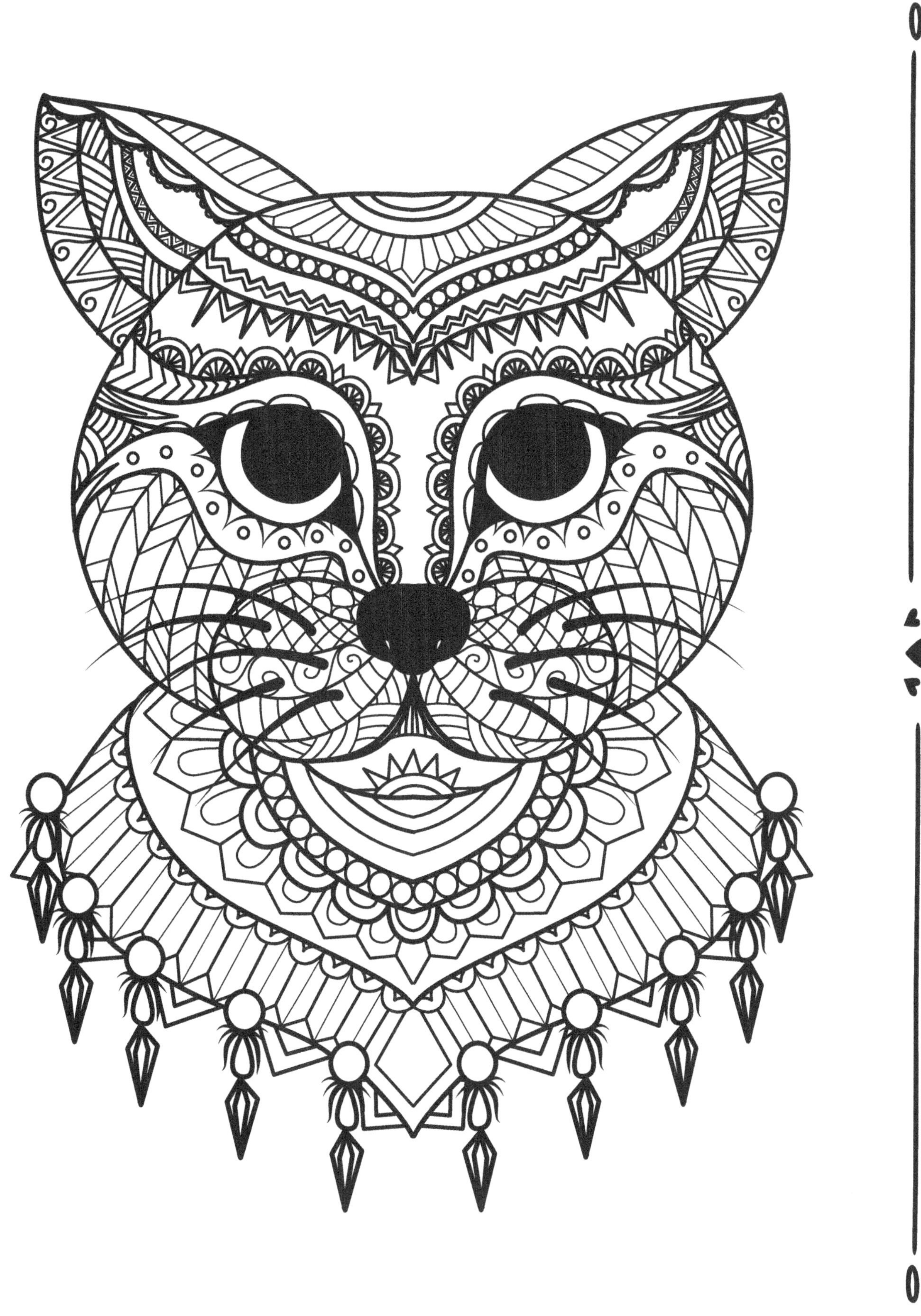

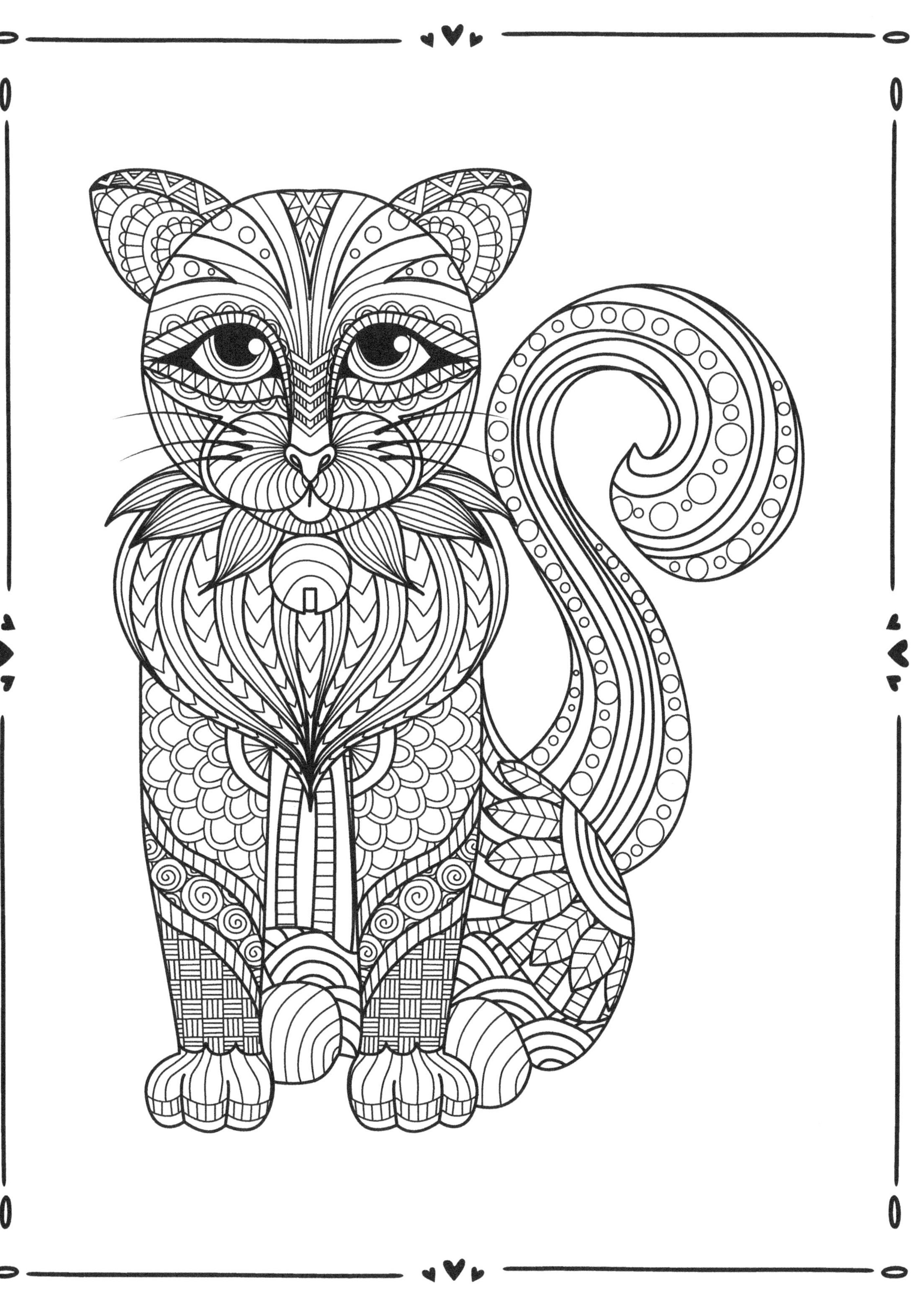

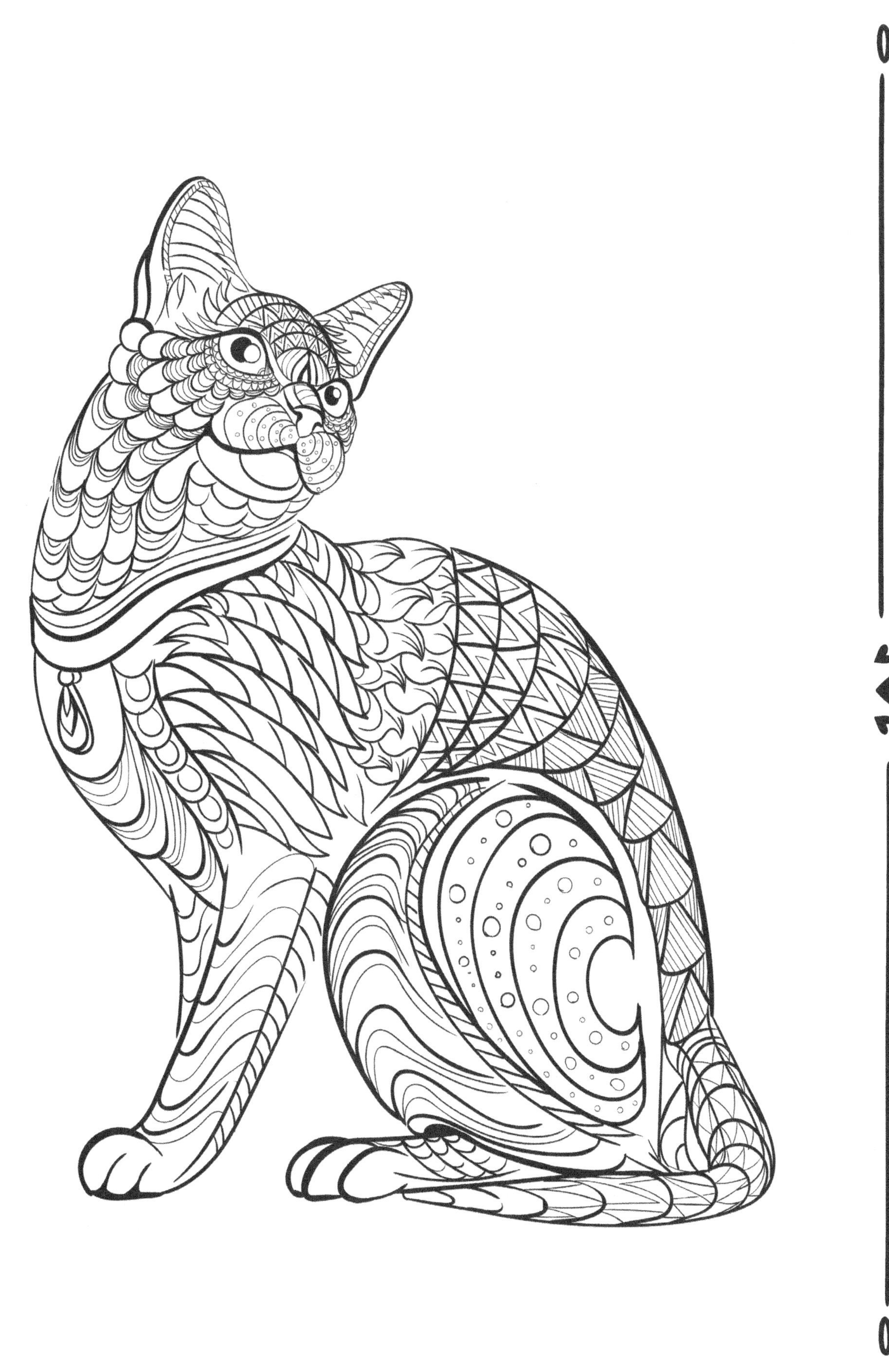

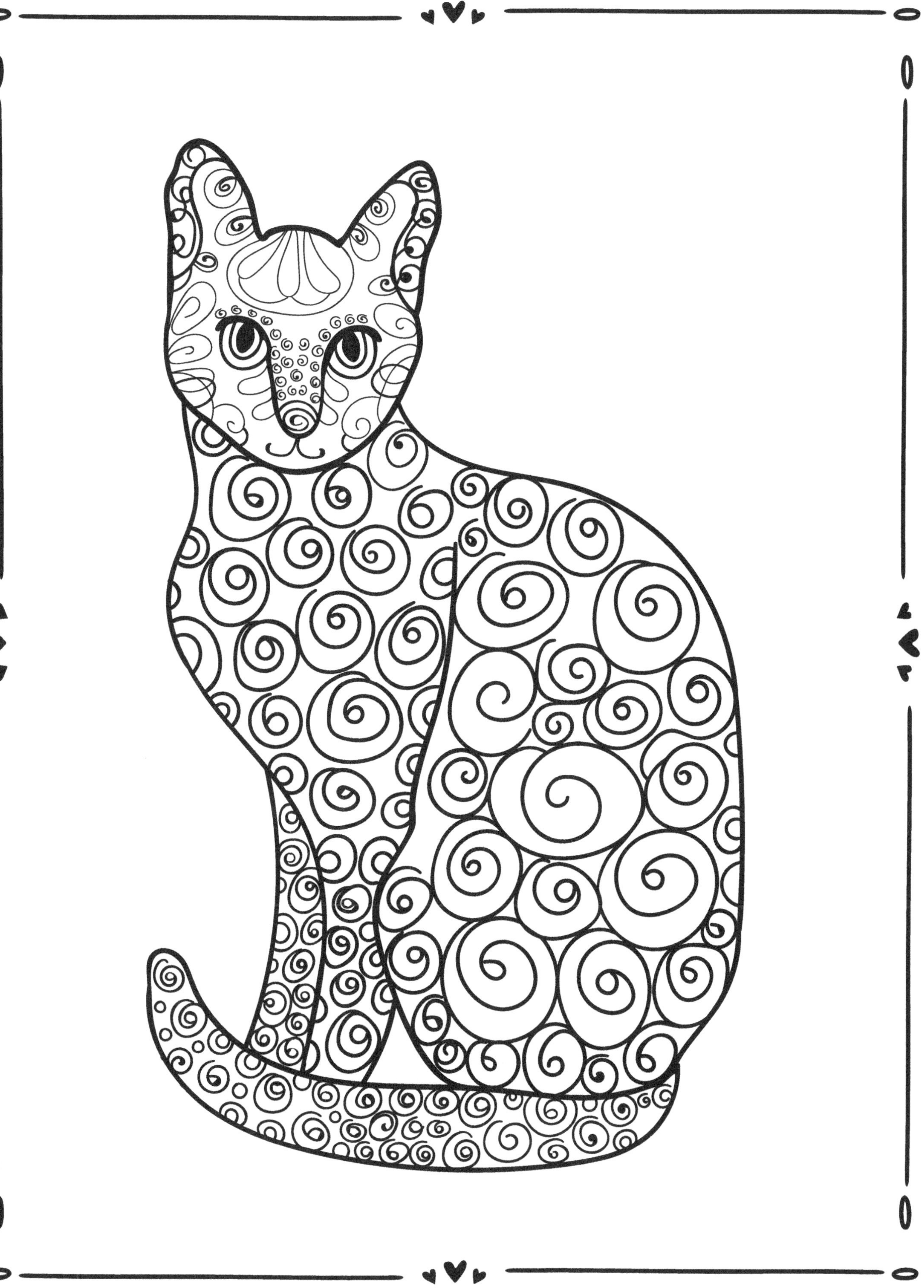

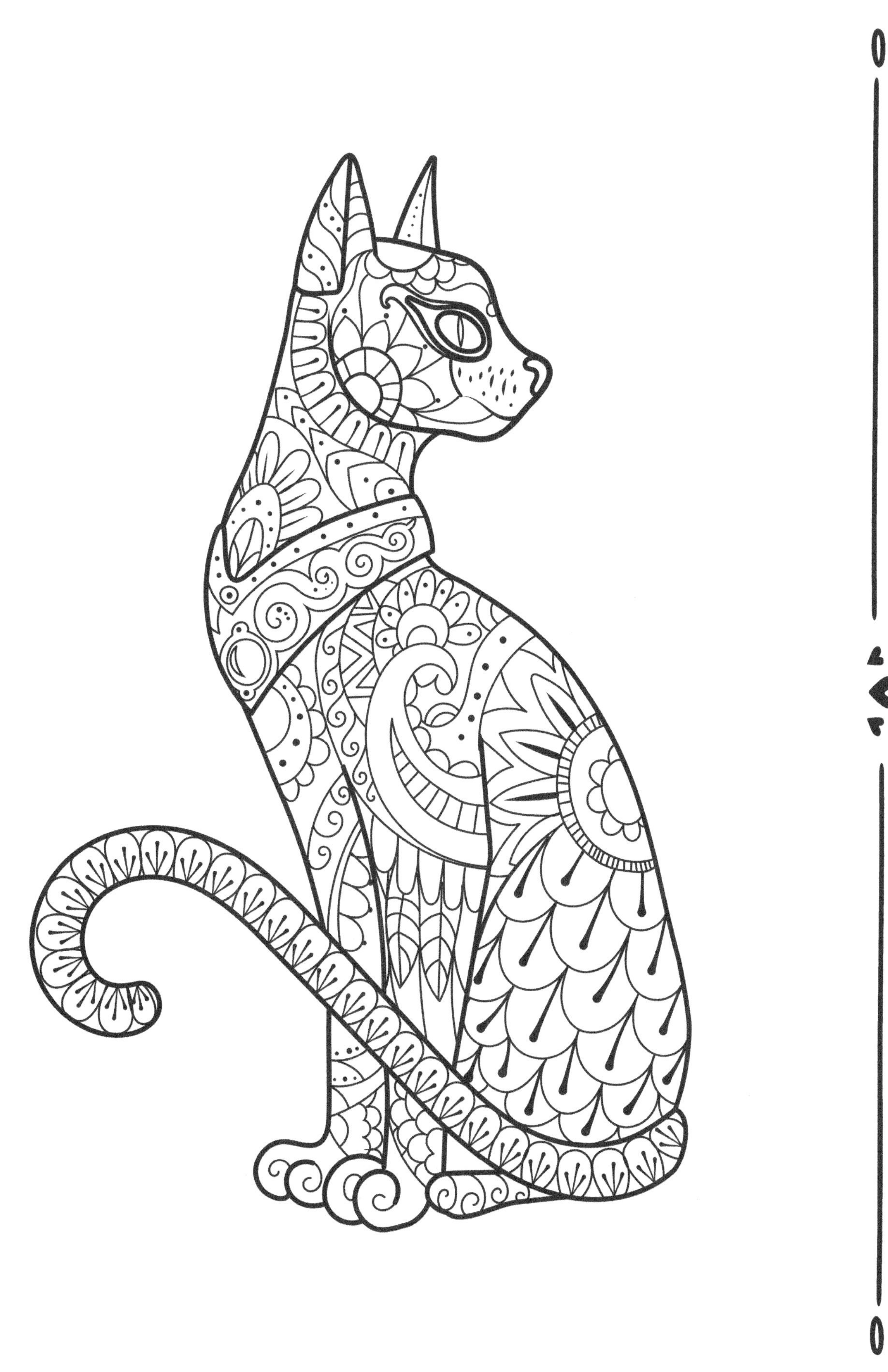

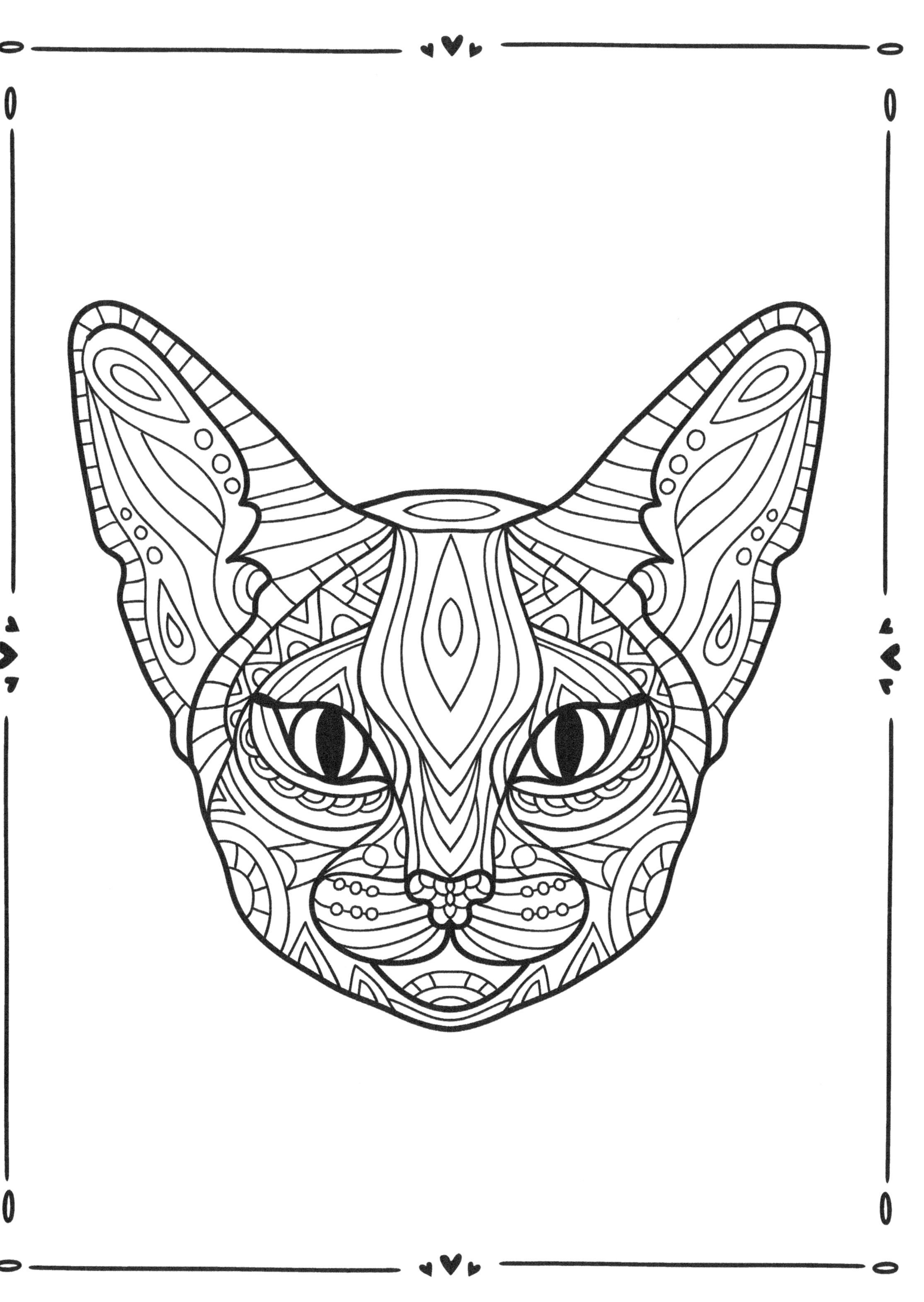

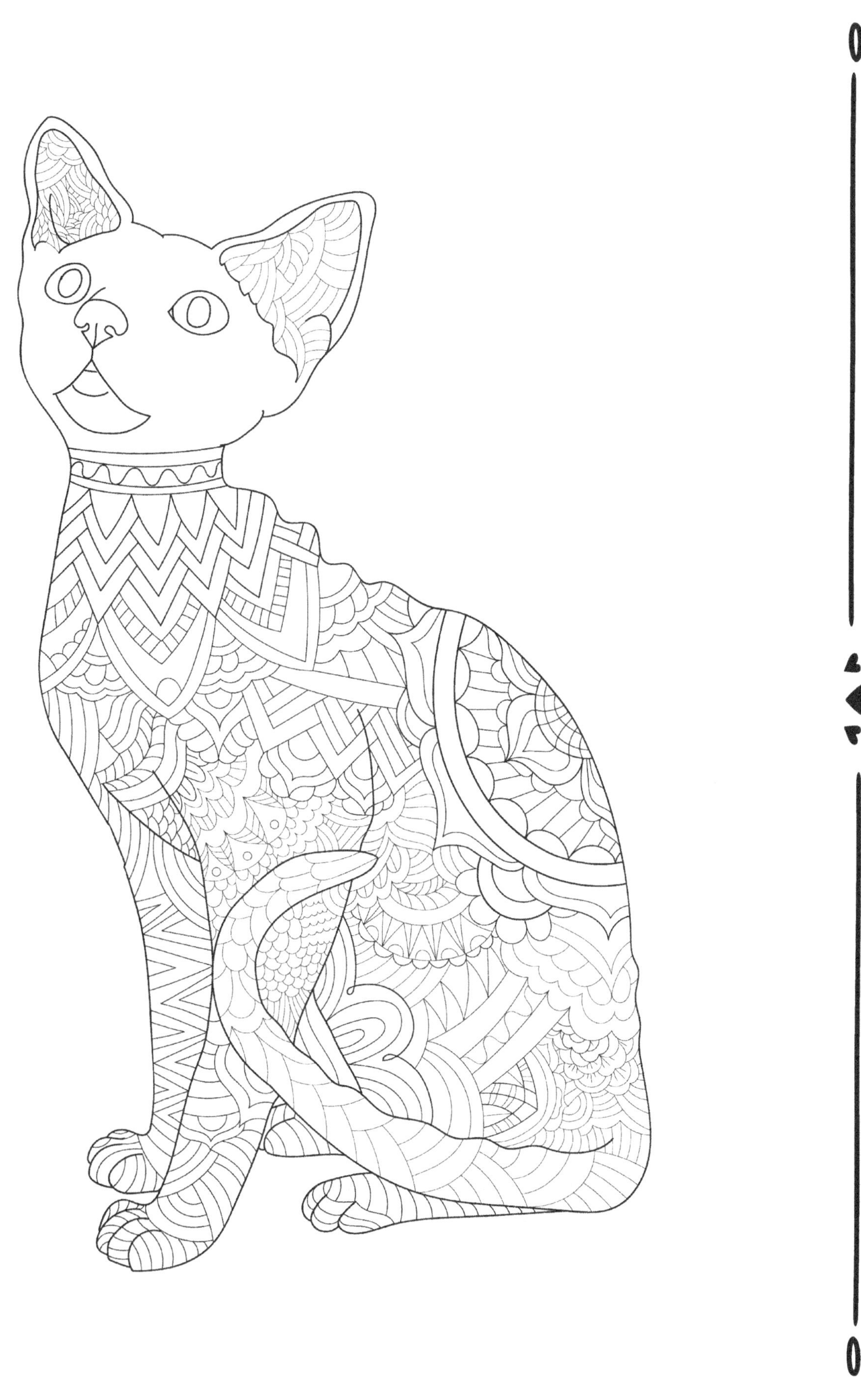

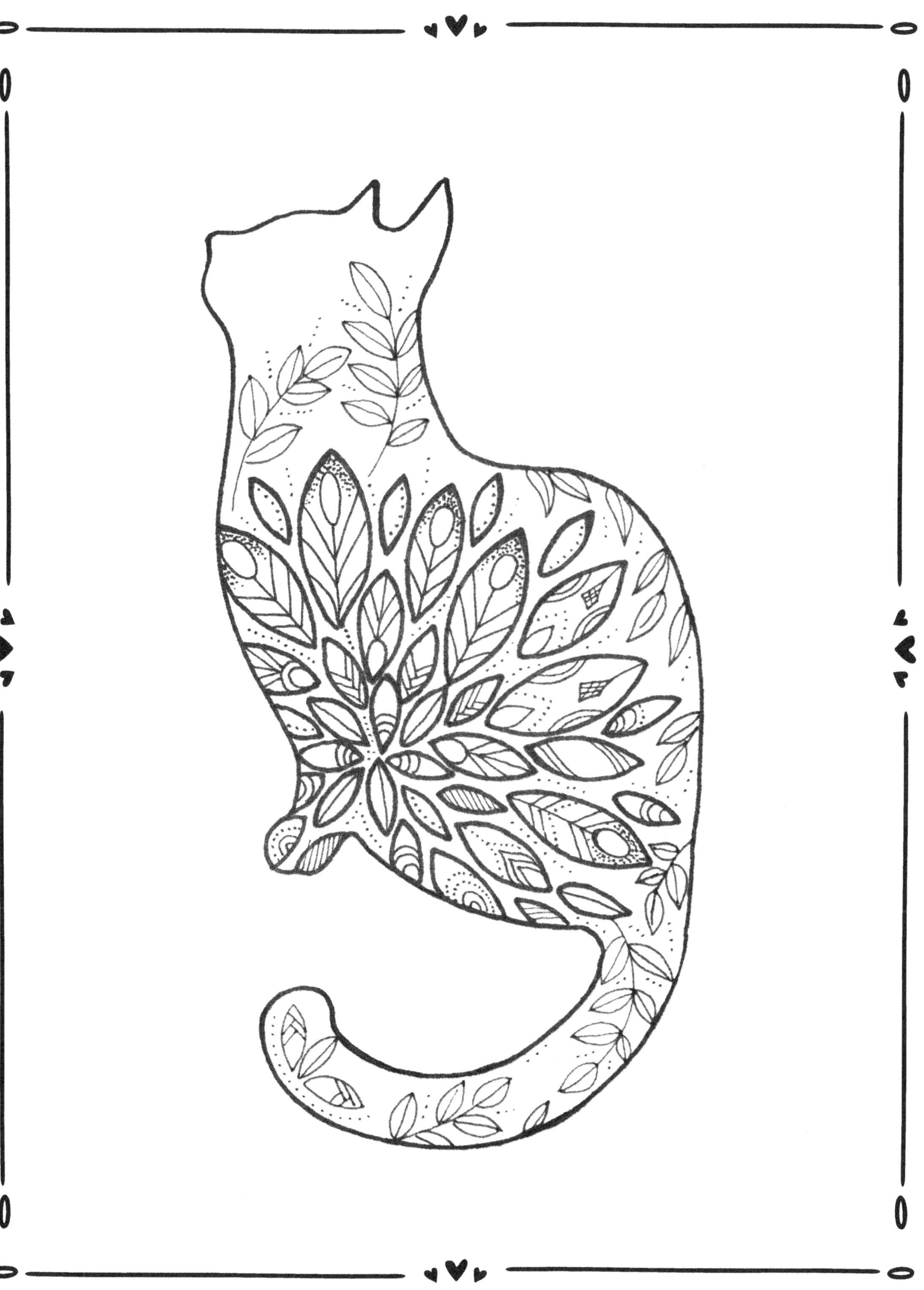

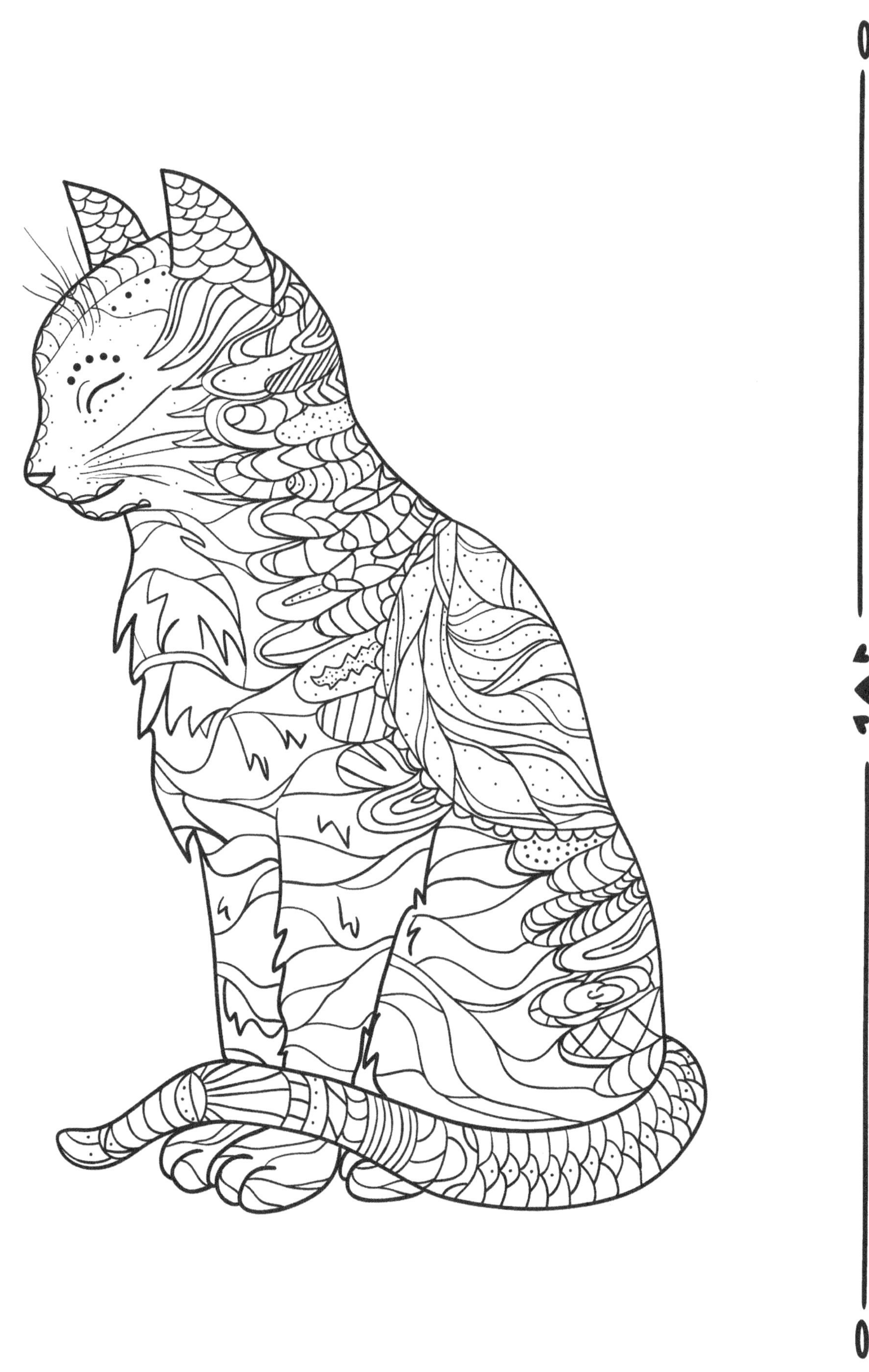

Made in the USA
Monee, IL
07 July 2026

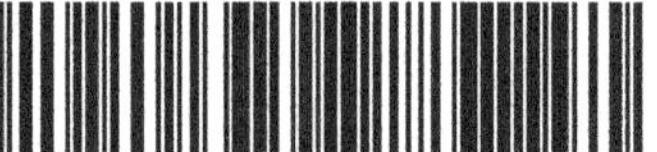

56545671R00037